Foreword by

CLAUDE HAMILTON

POINT AND GRUNT

Highly Effective Communication for Leaders and Teams

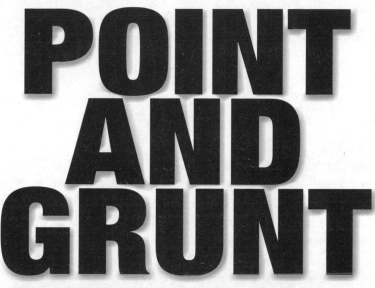

WHAT TO DO • WHAT NOT TO DO

OBSTACLÉS PRESS

D0683741

Life Leadership Essentials Series

First Edition, March 2016
10 9 8 7 6 5 4 3 2 1

Published by:

Obstaclés Press
200 Commonwealth Court
Cary, NC 27511

lifeleadership.com

ISBN 978-0-9971212-1-6

Cover design and layout by Norm Williams, nwa-inc.com

Printed in the United States of America

Successful communication is the exponential effect of little things done consistently over time…. A leader must inspire, or his team will expire.

—Chris Brady

CONTENTS

PART SIX: MEDIUMS OF COMMUNICATION

PART SEVEN: CHARACTER AND COMMUNICATION

FOREWORD
by Claude Hamilton

Point and Grunt is the kind of book that you will always want to keep close by to revisit throughout the year. Every time you read it, more secrets, new information, and additional keys to your success will be revealed.

Over the years, I have worked very hard to set many goals while putting in the legwork to achieve them. Whether it was in my past career in the military, in my marriage, raising my children, or especially in my twenty years as an entrepreneur, every breakthrough I've had was predicated by my improvement in communication. When I raised my influence and actually strived to become a better communicator, almost instantaneously there was a direct impact on my success. I can assure you that in life there isn't anything as valuable in any endeavor as becoming a better communicator.

When I met Orrin Woodward and Chris Brady I had already built a successful business, my marriage was flourishing, and we had a lot of great friends. I did have some success communicating, but I never purposely studied to grow and nurture my communication skills. What I learned from Orrin and Chris was that those skills would allow me to add value to others and help people attain the same success that I had worked so hard for. As I became a hungry student for the exact lessons that you will read about in *Point and Grunt*, I realized that I could grow much more and actually achieve goals that weren't even on my radar before I met them. I can only imagine what could happen if these essential principles were taught in school!

Point and Grunt covers all aspects of communication and does quite a brilliant job of connecting traditional and proven methods with the new frontiers of social media. I have read many books and worked diligently to learn the lessons that are compiled here in this single book. Not that I am suggesting, but you might never read another book on the art of dealing with others, and this book would completely cover you!

Chris and Orrin taught me that every and any business is about people, and the better you get at interacting with others, listening, apologizing, resolving conflict, explaining your ideas, building relationships, and generally serving others by communicating well, then the more successful you will become. I love the title of this book because it reminds me that at one point in my life, my level of communicating was a mixture of silence and really not much more than pointing and grunting!

Sincerely,
Claude Hamilton: Life Leadership Co-Founder
and author of *Toughen Up!*

INTRODUCTION

"Dare to live an excellent life."
—CHRIS BRADY & ORRIN WOODWARD

How Great Can You Be?

Communication is a big deal. But then, you already know that. In this book, you're going to learn how to communicate at a whole new level of effectiveness. This will have a huge positive impact in your life—at home, at work, and beyond.

Part One of this book introduces the topic, the overall category of communication, and shows how important it is. Parts Two through Seven give you practical, hands-on techniques and skills that will drastically improve your ability to powerfully communicate, whenever you need to. But before we move on to these important skills, it's essential to be very clear on how communication can make such a huge difference in our lives.

To do this, let's start by using your imagination....

You're in the movie *Night at the Museum: Secret of the Tomb*. Actually *in* it, like it's real life, or like you're there during the filming. Cool, right? You look around. The museum is even bigger in real life than in the movie. It's noisy, too. Is the monkey really allowed to make such a racket?

"Okay," you tell yourself, "I need to focus. I'm here for a reason."

You scan the warehouse. Larry Daley (aka Ben Stiller) is attempting to speak to the fictional Neanderthal version of himself, telling the caveman to stay where he is. "That Neanderthal is an amazing actor," you whisper to yourself. "Is he Ben Stiller too?" A cameraman glances at you, gesturing that you need to be quiet.

"I'm not nearly as noisy as the monkey," you tell yourself.

You edge closer, trying to hear every word....

Every time Larry gives the command to "stay," his caveman self nods in agreement, promising to do as he's told. Yet the moment Larry turns around to walk away, his caveman follows him, in direct opposition to the communication that just happened.

He points. He grunts. He nods. Then he does the opposite of the words. What kind of communication is this?

The Communication Quandary

Actually, it's fairly common in the world. Our communication isn't always what it should be. And if you're a leader or want to be a leader, this is a big problem.

Let's break this down even further, just to get the details right. Larry tells his caveman to do something. He's clear. He uses direct and simple words. He repeats himself. He uses his hands and gestures to reinforce his message. And the caveman listens, nods at exactly the right times, and agrees to obey.

But when Larry turns to leave, the caveman does precisely the opposite of what Larry said. Weird, right?

What's going on here?

What gives?

Like millions of managers, and billions and billions of parents across the world, you are stumped. Why don't the words — clear, direct words — translate into action? What's wrong with this picture?

What you might not yet realize — most people don't — is that communication is a category. Like food or cars. Or toast. Not so much like toast, actually. Toast is basically a subcategory of food.

Of all the categories, communication might be one of the most important, because all other categories will either benefit or suffer from a lack of effective communication.

Food is quite a category. It motivates lots of people to do lots of things on lots of days.

So does the category of communication.

More than cars, for that matter. Except maybe Ferraris. And Lamborghinis. And other Italian things.

But back to communication.

The caveman keeps following Larry rather than staying put, no matter how often they discuss the situation and agree on a mutually acceptable solution. This happens to a lot of people. It happens with the caveman several times before Larry finally convinces him to stay.

One of the Most Important

Business leader Chris Brady taught that, of all the categories, communication might be one of the most important, because all other categories will either benefit or suffer from a lack of effective communication. This applies to personal and professional life, to community and church, to finances and health. Really, Brady affirmed, it applies to all aspects of life. If you don't know how to effectively communicate, all other areas of your life will suffer.

But that's just the negative side of it. The more positive reality is that if you *do* know how to communicate well, all other areas of your life will be strengthened. It's hard to imagine any part of life that won't benefit from better communication.

> **If you're not effectively communicating, you will not be effectively working with other people—at least not as effectively as you could be.**

In fact, a perusal of world history provides numerous examples of great communication translating to great accomplishments. In Daniel Boorstin's famous world trilogy (*The Discovers, The Creators,* and *The Seekers*), communication is clearly an underlying foundation of success—for pioneers, inventors, discoverers, and other leaders.

In business, best-selling author Jim Collins shows that communication is a powerful means of turning *Good to Great*. Communication empowers innovators to turn new ideas into reforms, breakthroughs, and powerful revolutions that bless the world.

Nuance Can Change Everything

The point? If you're not effectively communicating, you will not be effectively working with other people — at least not as effectively as you could be. Communication is that important.

Communication influences practically everything. And becoming a better communicator means you'll improve almost every facet of your life. If you want to be a leader, becoming a good communicator, even a great communicator, is crucially important.

In this book, we'll learn 32 rules of effective, quality, excellent communication. As leaders, or potential leaders, we can try to just point and grunt when we have something to communicate, hoping that we get our point across to other people more often than not.

The truth is that a lot of people try this approach.

But there is a better way. A more effective way. And it is actually quite simple:

Learn and apply these 32 rules.

They work. They're simple. And it won't take long to learn them. But without them, your communication will always be less than it could be.

Note that we have no desire to turn this into another textbook on the topic of communication, of which there are many. Instead, our focus is on 32 key, hard-hitting rules of communication that will help you quickly and effectively increase your leadership skills by being a better communicator.

Our purpose is to introduce these rules and help you apply them, so you can use them to immediately, and in many cases drastically, improve your communication skills, boost the quality of important relationships, upgrade your leadership abilities, and improve your life.

Leader Voice

As best-selling author Marcus Buckingham wrote: "Great leaders rally people to a better future."[1] What a great definition! In fact, it's worth rereading, just to be sure you get the full importance and meaning:

> *"Great leaders rally people to a better future."*

According to Buckingham, any other definition of leadership falls short.[2] If you don't rally people to a better future, whatever you're doing isn't really leadership.

Of course, such rallying won't happen without the right kind of communication. Period.

This is real. If you want to lead, you have to be able to rally people to a better future, and this means you need to communicate effectively.

Interestingly, Buckingham compared *management* to *leadership* by suggesting that a great manager is one who works individually with each person to bring out his or her best, unique talents and skills in order to achieve top performance.[3] When this is done with numerous individuals in a group, they become a team.

But what makes this kind of truly excellent management work? You guessed it. This requires great communication.

To summarize: How does a manager work with individuals to help each of them truly increase the quality of their performance each week, month, and year? And how does a leader truly rally those he serves to a better future, and to consistently

> **If you want to lead, you have to be able to rally people to a better future, and this means you need to communicate effectively.**

and enthusiastically do the hard and sustained work that is necessary to actually build such a future?

A huge part of the answer is communication. Indeed, without great communication, none of this is going to happen, no matter what else the leaders and managers bring to the table. And learning to apply the 32 rules in this book wisely and effectively will powerfully boost your communication skills.

Oh, The Places You'll Go

Indeed, as Chris Brady put it, "How you communicate will have a lot to do with how far you go in life."[4] Brady went on to teach that your level of communication skills will directly influence whether, how often, and at what levels you:

- get hired
- stay employed
- get promoted
- get asked on dates
- get told "yes" when you ask someone on a date
- obtain funding for your company
- succeed in business
- effectively lead
- make important sales

The list goes on. Moreover, in Brady's words: "It will largely determine how people end up framing their views about you. It will also largely determine whether you are a person who is known for solving problems or creating them."

Communication Is You

In short, to a large extent, your communication *is* you.

Think about that for a moment. The only way other people can know you is through your communication — of one kind or another. Communication is the bridge between us all. As Paul J. Meyer put it: "Communication — the human connection—is the key to personal and career success."

Clearly, communication is incredibly important.

That's what this book is all about. We're going to dig into the exciting category of communication and help elevate the movie

The only way other people can know you is through your communication.

of your life to a whole new and better level.

But don't for a minute forget that this is also going to be *fun!*

Just tune out the jabbering monkeys, strap on your parachute, and get ready to elevate your communication skills to new heights. This one change will help in pretty much every part of your life. Get out your pen, put away the *Night at the Museum* DVD, tell your inner caveman or cavewoman to actually follow you this time, point and grunt as much as necessary to get really fired up about lifting your communication skills to new and better levels, and let's jump right in....

PART ONE

THE IMPORTANCE OF COMMUNICATION

"Wise men speak because they have something to say; fools because they have to say something."
—PLATO

TREAT COMMUNICATION AS A VERY IMPORTANT CATEGORY!

*"The single biggest problem in communication is
the illusion that it has taken place."*
—GEORGE BERNARD SHAW

Who Stole The Money

Perhaps Chris Brady said it best when he shared the example of various different things that can be communicated with the simple phrase "I did not say he stole the money."

Even without adding punctuation and simply emphasizing specific words, there are as many meanings to this sentence as there are words! Nuance is important.

Try it out for yourself! Go through this sentence delightfully emphasizing a different word each time, and just watch what happens:

"*I* did not say he stole the money."
"I did *not* say he stole the money."
"I did not *say* he stole the money."

This is crazy, right? The same words communicate very different things. By the way, this kind of interesting pattern is even less pronounced in English or German than it would be in Italian, Spanish, or Portuguese. Why? Because in these last three languages native speakers would likely add very different and at times highly animated hand gestures to each of these sentences. In Chinese there would be an even larger disparity between the ways these different meanings are pronounced, because the speaker would often use an entirely different tone of voice.

And guess what, the further you go with this, the more numerous and different the individual meanings become! For example:

> "I did not say *he* stole the money."
> "I did not say he *stole* the money."
> "I did not say he stole the *money*."

Practically every word in this sentence—when emphasized—creates its own distinct meaning, without changing anything else. You can even push this to extremes, by actually allowing every single word to take over the sentence:

> "I *did* not say he stole the money."
> "I did not say he stole *the* money."

It Deserves Your Respect

Communication is an important category, and leaders treat it that way!

In short, communication isn't as simple or easy as many people think. It's an entire category of knowledge, and it is a very important category to really understand. If you don't master the art of communication, this lack will always hold you back.

So that's the first rule: Communication is an important category, and leaders treat it that way! They respect it. They study communication and learn more about it whenever the opportunity arises. The best leaders keep learning how to improve their communication skills throughout

Leadership demands that you learn about communication, practice it, and master it.

their lives. They never reach a point where they decide, "Okay, that's it. I'm a perfect communicator. I don't need to work on it anymore."

Take Action

Leadership demands that you learn about communication, practice it, and master it. This is our starting point. Get excited about communication, and always treat it like it should be treated: as a very important category, topic, idea, and set of skills. Turn communication into one of your core interests, studies, and passions.

Even if you think you're not very good at communicating, this rule is very important. And again, if you think you are actually a pretty decent communicator, you can still do better. Communication is extremely important. Treat it that way!

RULE #2

ALWAYS REMEMBER THAT COMMUNICATION CAN BE A STICKY BUSINESS

*"Take advantage of every opportunity
to practice your communication skills...."*
—JIM ROHN

Relationships, Relationships...

Leaders take note. There are many factors involved in real communication and many ways to mess it all up. But when you get it right, miracles can happen.

Hearts can be touched, and hearts can be changed. Ideas can transform a person's life, and words or symbols can turn good to bad or mediocre to great. Communication is a sort of magic, or power, that can have a great positive—or negative—influence on people. On you. On those you love. On those you work with. On everyone.

In short, communication deeply, *deeply* matters.

If you don't remember to get the communications right, it can create all kinds of sticky or downright destructive problems.

The bottom line is, if you and your family or team aren't communicating well, any effectiveness that happens to occur is likely just coincidental. This is true in business, marriage, families, education, media, leadership, community, politics (just visit Washington or Ottawa sometime and watch a congressional or parliamentary session), and every other arena of life.

Anytime there is a *relationship*, communication is needed for things to run smoothly or for people to achieve success together. No matter how committed your team or family members, no matter how hard they work, no matter how well trained they are in other things,

> **If you and your family or team aren't communicating well, any effectiveness that happens to occur is likely just coincidental.**

poor communication can ruin everything you are trying to accomplish. Ineffective communication can destroy marriages, businesses, communities, and even nations.

A Few Practical Examples

For example, when Chinese government officials from the cities stopped understanding the common language of the farmers and villagers, the whole nation suffered. At first, the *mandarins* (a Chinese word denoting government "officials") looked down on the people in the *cantons* (meaning local areas), and as the Mandarin and Cantonese languages grew further apart, so did the values and viewpoints of these two segments of the nation.

Eventually they split, after a terrible civil war. Today the country of China officially speaks Mandarin, while the separate nation of Taiwan primarily speaks Cantonese. Not understanding each other can be a recipe for problems.

A similar kind of divide happened in the United States in the decades before the Civil War. People in the North and South used similar words, but certain words and phrases sometimes had very different meanings. The same occurred in Britain and the American colonies just before the Revolutionary conflict. For example, after a certain skirmish in the Boston Harbor in the early 1770s, references to tea meant something very different in America than in England.

In Britain, "tea" was a call to connect, interact, and bond. Across the Atlantic in the American colonies, it meant tyranny, monarchy, and fighting for freedom. That's a very big difference.

This kind of "communication disconnect" also occurred before the War of the Roses, and the list goes on and on.... There are practically as many other examples as there are wars.

The Main Point

So what are leaders supposed to do about such divides and divisions? Put simply: Don't ever forget that communication is extremely powerful. Make sure you think about how things are communicated, long *before* they become a problem.

When you are hiring people or training them or motivating or instructing, think about communication. Work the right kind of communication into your projects, plans, and relationships right from the beginning.

- Are you changing your sales training? Give a lot of thought to communication.
- Is your department expanding? Give a lot of thought to why, how, when, where, and who.
- Has a problem arisen? Don't just think about how to solve it; also consider how to communicate it most honestly and effectively.

In these and every other facet of leadership and relationships, getting the communication right will make a hugely positive difference. Getting it wrong, on the other hand, can do lots of damage.

When you encounter communication mistakes, be one of the leaders who helps create the solution.

Like Elephants

The best leaders never forget this key point. Indeed, top leaders consistently remember: Communication Can Be a Sticky Business, so give it your best effort, and reliably do what is needed to get it right. Likewise, when you encounter communication mistakes, be one of the leaders who helps create the solution.

Always be on the lookout for ways to improve your personal and organizational communication.

This is a vitally important rule.

RULE #3

LEADERS WHO WANT TO COMMUNICATE EFFECTIVELY MUST KNOW THEIR AUDIENCE

"I was born, and then I succeeded!"
—KIRK BIRTLES

Epic Truths

The importance of knowing your audience is one of the recurring themes in the greatest books of history. For example, Odysseus learns this lesson repeatedly in his travels, chronicled by Homer in the *Odyssey*. In differing cultures, and even among different social groups within a society, language and communication differences can cause numerous challenges.

SIDEBAR TO READER:

Westerners have been known to take this to extremes. For example, consider the following counsel from Winston Churchill:

"If you have an important point to make, don't try to be subtle or clever. Use a pile driver. Hit the point once. Then come back and hit it again. Then hit it a third time—a tremendous whack."

That's good advice, if you are communicating to other Westerners.

Different Strokes

But in some Asian cultures, and certain tribal societies in Africa and Latin America, boldness is considered proof of insecurity and weakness. Leaders speak quietly and humbly. Only low-level managers use boldness, and then only when they are desperate.

Likewise, in the West it is usually best to try to communicate your thoughts and ideas as clearly as possible, but in some Mediterranean nations, some cultures in the Middle East, China, and the countries of the Indonesian archipelago, riddles, poetry, subtleties, and hidden meanings are considered much more clear than direct statements. The tradition in these cultures is that direct statements must be lies, because a speaker or leader would only avoid using riddles or symbols if he is trying to hide something behind his bluntness—and such directness will almost always be questioned, analyzed, dissected, and challenged.

A good classic primer on this Eastern model, for leaders who may be developing teams or relationships in Asia, is the *Oedipus* trilogy by Sophocles. In short, culture is central to building effective relationships. It is essential to know your audience and to speak to them in a way that allows communication to actually happen.

Know Your Audience

Note that in this book we'll focus on communication to Western audiences, primarily general business and professional audiences.

But whatever other rule(s) you are applying to communication, always remember to

Know your audience, and communicate accordingly.

target it as necessary to your actual audience for any given communication. If you miss this, your communications can fall flat or, worse, offend or incite. Know your audience, and communicate accordingly.

If you are speaking, writing, talking directly, posting online, or otherwise communicating with an audience whose culture is unfamiliar, do a little research beforehand. A bit of digging now can drastically increase your effectiveness—and it may save you from major efforts attempting to fix things later. Just showing the group that you are trying hard to respect their culture will go a long way if you do slip up here and there.

Even within your own culture, with people you are comfortable addressing, take time to think about your audience before important communications. What do they need right now? What do they need most from you? How can you best help them? What are they expecting, and how will they react to your planned communications?

Again, know your audience, and take a bit of time to consider them before communicating. This is a crucial element of effective leadership.

RULE #4

SEEK TO MASTER THE SKILL OF COMMUNICATION

"Good communication is just as stimulating as black coffee, and just as hard to sleep after."
—ANNE MORROW LINDBERGH

Mastery

With the understanding that communication is a very important category, can sometimes be a sticky business, and changes at times depending on the audience you are interacting with, it's pretty easy to see why communication is so crucial for perspective leaders. Put another way, top leaders know *Rule #4: Seek to Master the Skills of Communication.*

The key word in Rule #4 is *master*. It's not enough to just dabble at this. Top leaders go much further. And mastery takes practice, progress, and experience.

Chris Brady emphasized this when he taught that successful communication goes well beyond just a single principle or idea. It is more than just a subject or field of knowledge. The scope and scale of ineffective communication can be devastating at times—because everything we say could potentially communicate as many meanings as there are people and words.

Moreover, since the right kind of communication can significantly increase success in almost any endeavor, effective communication is needed to bridge the gap between individuals, teams, and ideas.

Back to the Movies

That's deep. So with a basic understanding of these first few principles, let's get back to your acting career. You suddenly find yourself in the movie *Hoodwinked*. You're standing in a forest. The trees are tall, and the animals speak English. "This is pretty radical," you tell yourself, if you were born in the fifties or sixties. If you're a little bit younger you say, "Awesome!"

> **Communication is what gets us all on the same page so that the story can come together in a meaningful and powerful way.**

You look around warily, because you know the Big Bad Wolf is lurking somewhere in the woods.

The director yells, "Action!" and the other actors start acting. They're all animated, but you pay close attention to every word. You are still scanning the underbrush in case the Wolf comes along, so you're not sure who says it, but the words strike a chord in your mind.

"If a tree falls in the forest," the voice affirms, "there will be at least three stories: yours, mine and the tree's." You nod, and you start to ponder....

There are many different viewpoints, and as we've said, communication is what gets us all on the same page so that the story can come together in a meaningful and powerful way. Everyone learns more, and we all adopt a shared meaning and purpose. Even if there is disagreement, effective communication helps us share a common experience of thinking and learning.

High Stakes

In times of crisis, such as war, famine, disease, or economic struggle, the quality of a nation's communication can make all the difference. The majority if not all of the world's problems are made more difficult when there is a lack of—or downright bad—communication.

Now, since we're on the topic of mastery, let's zoom in on your movie. Not somebody else's movie this time (like *Night at the Museum* or *Hoodwinked*) but rather the story of *your* life.

Yes, *you*. Please don't look around to see what actors are preparing for the shoot. Ben Stiller isn't here. The characters aren't animated, and there is no screaming monkey or morose person dressed like a Neanderthal around (unless that's something you regularly experience most days).

It's just you and your real life.

And here's a very important lesson: Your level of communication skill (or lack thereof) is going to make a huge difference in your life. This is a big deal. Rule #4 is very, very important.

But How?

Now, note that mastery isn't as easy as it might seem at first blush. After all, how many true master communicators are there around?

The truth is that there are actually quite a few. None of them is perfect, of course, but you can probably think of at least five to ten or so people who are really good communicators. They move you. They know how to teach you in a way that makes you sit up and really take notice.

> **If you master the communication skills of leadership, you'll be a true leader and a master communicator.**

Or they talk to you in a way that is truly uplifting. Or motivating. Or…fill in the blank.

Such communicators are approaching mastery, at least of certain communication skills, and some of them are real masters in their own right. This gives us a key, a powerful hint about how to actually master the communication skills you want and need to fulfill your goals and life purpose.

The key is simply this: To master something, emulate those who have already mastered it. Listen to them. Learn from them. Seek their wisdom. Apply what they teach. Practice it, and then return and learn more from them.

Keep up this process of seeking, listening, learning, and practicing until you are, yourself, a master of the skills you seek.

> **To master something, emulate those who have already mastered it. Listen to them. Learn from them. Seek their wisdom.**

Sounds simple, right? Actually, it usually requires a lot of hard work. But it's worth it. If you master the communication skills of leadership, you'll be a true leader and a master communicator. That's what the rules in this book are all about: learning from great communicators, so you can become such a leader yourself. We'll dig deeper into this as we move along through the remaining rules.

BONUS

ALWAYS REMEMBER THE BASICS

*"Help enough other people get what they want
and you'll have everything you want."*
—ZIG ZIGLAR

Don't Forget!

As you read this book, we'll introduce many additional important principles, but first let's briefly review the four introductory rules we've already covered, and find ways to start applying them in our daily communication. These first four rules of great communication may seem very basic—because they are.

They are, in fact, foundational, and vital to quality and effective communication. If you want to be a great communicator, it is essential to remember these four basics:

*Rule #1: Treat Communication as a Very
Important Category!*

Applying this guideline begins by accepting that it's true. But this is a big step for some people. Still, this is very important. Communication really is of major importance for everyone, especially for leaders, and it deserves our attention and focus! Top leaders make it a lifetime priority.

Rule #2: Always Remember that Communication Can Be a Sticky Business

This means that getting your communications right is worth the effort, but it won't just happen unless you make it a priority.

Rule #3: Leaders Who Want to Communicate Effectively Must Know Their Audience

Many of the rules can shift on a dime when you move from one audience to another. Always know enough about your audience to communicate effectively.

Rule #4: Seek to Master *the Skills of Communication*

Top leaders aren't content with their current level of communication skills. They want to improve. Maintaining this view and drive throughout your life is an important leadership skill, and the other skills that will come from continually trying to upgrade your mastery will be a blessing to you and many others. The best way to master communication is to learn from master communicators. That's the focus of the rules in this book.

PART TWO

MASTER THE
BIG FIXES

"The two words 'information' and 'communication' are often used interchangeably, but they signify quite different things.

"Information is giving out; communication is getting through."
—SYDNEY J. HARRIS

BE PROFESSIONAL

*"A person who does not value your time
will not value your advice."*
—ORRIN WOODWARD

Big Picture

Now that we've learned and are hopefully beginning to apply the four basics from Part One, let's focus on what master communicator Chris Brady calls "the big picture stuff." As he explained: "These are really just loose concepts to think about. None of these will really surprise you…. None of this is all that earth-shattering, but usually it's more helpful to be reminded than it is to be instructed.

"If you knew everything you should know by now, you wouldn't need to learn anything new. If you knew everything you've already forgotten, you wouldn't need much more." In other words, you probably already know many of the things on the list below, but keep your eyes open anyway and find ways to incorporate these "big picture" guidelines into your communication. They will help immensely.

Besides, as the old saying goes, "To know, and not to *do*, is not to know." Practice applying the following principles of excellent communication more often and more effectively.

This Is Big!

Our next rule is hugely important:

Rule #5: Be Professional

You've almost certainly heard this recommendation before, but it really is one of the most important principles of communication. Indeed, being professional plays a *central* role in effective communication. It's definitely a "Big Fix." If you take the time to develop your professionalism, you may be surprised at how quickly and effectively you improve in other communication skills. If you plan to be a leader, professionalism is a must. This is especially true in business, but it applies to all facets of life.

The Definition

Professionalism means to doing things the way your colleagues and customers would expect if you were the most successful person in the world at what you do. When you communicate professionally, it usually brings everyone you deal with up to a more professional level.

> **Communication should carry a heavy dose of your personality, a strong sense of who you really are.**

It also says something about you, and about whatever business or organization you represent. Professionalism is meeting the standard of interaction and integrity of the best leaders and the most effective organizations on the planet.

A Deeper Definition

Moreover, when you are professional, you are a "pro." People can count on you. They know you stand for something. They know you'll do things right, even when it's hard. And they know you'll do the right things.

When you are not professional, all of this comes into question. Who are you? What can they depend on? What should they expect? Leaving those you work with (and work for) in doubt on such things will only hurt your business and tend to block your success. Professionalism makes a huge difference.

The Fun

Another way to say "professionalism" is "consistency at the highest standard."

Of course, professional doesn't have to mean "not fun." There can be fun within almost any professional boundaries. Proper communication should carry a heavy dose of your personality, a strong sense of who you really are. And fun is part of success. So is humor. But professionalism and fun are partners, not enemies. They should go together.

Remember that your professionalism—or lack of it—is clearly communicating something about you at all times and to everyone you meet.

Including fun in your daily work is essential, and it doesn't mean there's never a time to be serious. That's the whole point of being professional. Communicating professionally means knowing *when* to laugh, *when* to have fun, and *when* to buckle down and be serious. Professionals do both.

Make the Choice

Moreover, pretty much everyone recognizes unprofes-

sionalism when they see it. If you are behaving, speaking, or interacting in a way that is inappropriate, even a little, you are not being professional. That's the key to professionalism: always be appropriate to the circumstance.

> **Another way to say "professionalism" is "consistency at the highest standard."**

This concept doesn't need a lot of extra commentary. You either choose to be professional, or you don't. But remember that your professionalism—or lack of it—is clearly communicating something about you at all times and to everyone you meet.

RULE #6

BE CLEAR, PART I

"Effective communication is 20 percent what you know and 80 percent how you feel about what you know."
—Jim Rohn

What Font Are You Speaking In?

Another essential key to effective communication is to follow *Rule #6: Communication Needs To Be Clear*. This is a very important part of communicating, and it is one of the true "Big Fixes" in communication. Be clear.

Every top leader experiences receiving what Chris Brady calls "inscrutable e-mails." For example, what would you think if you opened your e-mail today and read the following:

Hi. I are happy to e-mail me?

You're thinking: "Huh? What?"
"Why?"
It's probably just a typo, so no harm done. But what if such a confusing e-mail is really important? What if, let's say, it comes from one of your main contacts, and reads:

The supplier can't deliver this month. The no refund policy is not an exception. When meeting?

"Uh… What on earth?"
Is this e-mail trying to communicate that the supplier can't meet your order this month and you won't get a refund? Or that you won't get your order but you *will* get a refund?
The funny thing is that the true meaning was probably pretty clear to the person who wrote it. He knows whether you're getting a refund or not. But you have no idea.
Beyond that, what's the part about a meeting? Does the e-mail communicate that the person wants to meet with you about this issue? Or about something else? Or does the person want to meet with someone else—like the supplier or maybe whoever sets refund policies? Or are

the supplier and the setter of refund policies supposed to meet? Who are "they" in this cryptic message? Was this e-mail even meant for you?

A Deeper Look

The person who wrote this e-mail probably wants to meet with you. Maybe. Or…not. It's actually unclear.

Brady's word *inscrutable* is the only thing to call this kind of communiqué.

Yet, again, the person who wrote it is probably sure that he has clearly communicated. And he is likely waiting to hear back from you on this important issue.

What are you supposed to do? Send a reply that simply says, "What???"

It's just plain confusing.

The sad reality is that this kind of poor communication happens a lot. And it is a serious problem, at least if you want to actually communicate.

Another example. You get a text from your daughter during the school day:

> plans changed pickup time won't
> work 4pm with chelsea see ya lol XD

Okay. So let's decipher this bit of ancient Sanskrit. Your daughter has changed her plans. But is she getting a ride with Chelsea to your home, or is she going to Chelsea's house? Maybe they're going to the mall. Or is she still expecting a ride from you?

Is the new pickup time 4 pm? Or is 4 pm the time she's hanging out with Chelsea? (Probably that one.) (Maybe.)

Are you supposed to pick up both her and Chelsea? What does XD mean? Does "see ya" mean "see you later when you pick me up," or "see you later since I don't need you to pick me up"?

If you know your daughter's electronic shorthand, you probably have a pretty good idea what she's saying. But if you don't, good luck.

Either way, your daughter is probably sure she's clearly communicated with you.

The truth is that almost everyone has experienced e-mails or messages with communication barriers like those in the examples above. Sometimes a person asks a question that doesn't make any sense. Or maybe you ask *them* three questions, and they answer with a simple "yes." But which question were they answering?

SIDEBAR TO READER:

Remember the following great exchange in the classic movie *The Princess Bride*?

Vizzini: "He didn't fall? Inconceivable!"

Iñigo Montoya: "You keep using that word. I do not think it means what you think it means."

Avoid This!

Of course, it's one thing to receive such messages and not know how to respond to them. It's another thing to *be* the one who sent them.

Don't do this!

Your communication certainly isn't at its finest if other people only see your words as "inscrutable e-mails," "inscrutable texts," "inscrutable voice messages," "inscrutable posts," or any other "inscrutable" kind of communication.

For that matter, "inconceivable" communications aren't good either.

The solution is simple: Be clear. If communication is needed, it's worth taking the extra second or two to make sure your words actually mean what you think they mean. In short, you should almost always try to refrain from using "purple prose" and making your language so flowery that it's hard to understand.

Keep It Simple

Direct and simple communication is nearly always better. For example, let's consider the following two ways of getting drivers to slow down in a subdivision:

Option One: Printed on a Flyer and Delivered to Each Home

ATTENTION!!!

Too many drivers drive too fast in this subdivision, and this lack of attention to the Codes and Covenants of the Development is causing undue danger to the various inhabitants of the area, particularly those who are minors. This has come to the attention of the Community Board and we are very concerned about the possible ramifications of continued disregard of these important guidelines by those who traverse our streets.

Because of this situation, the Board has voted to respond to this problem in various ways. First, any driver caught going faster than the posted limits will be given extra fines on their annual community dues, as authorized per section 9.2(d) of the CCR's of the Development. This is non-negotiable.

Second, if the behavior continues, we will be forced to take further actions. Since this concerns everyone in this Community, we have determined not to extend penalties without letting everyone take part in the decision-making process on this policy and its particulars. A special hearing will be held on March 23 to discuss other remedies. All homeowners are invited to participate. At the conclusion of the hearing, the Community Board will make a final vote on this issue.

Option Two: Posted as a Sign at Strategic Places on the Roads

Speed Bump Ahead
SLOW DOWN!
Fines Enforced

Clearly the first option is long, confusing, inflamma-tory, and bureaucratic. In fact, such flyers in real life are often three or four times this long, and they say just as little. Also, just for clarity, is the Committee in the first flyer fining speeders or not? They say yes, then they say maybe. It's unclear.

The whole point is just to tell everyone to slow down. So why not be direct and clear? Communication is much more effective when it is brief and simple.

Top leaders learn that it is nearly always a mistake to word things in a way that is hard to understand. It is much more effective to make questions clear and statements understandable.

> **"The ability to simplify means to eliminate the unnecessary so that the necessary may speak."**

Again, as we learned in Part One, how you communicate is critical.

Hans Hoffman wisely said, "The ability to simplify means to eliminate the unnecessary so that the necessary may speak." Communication is often simplification. Eliminate the unnecessary so that the really important things can be understood clearly.

RULE #7

BE CLEAR, PART II

"You will not feel most energized and challenged when focusing on your flaws."
—MARCUS BUCKINGHAM

"Give the Dog a Good Name"

The phrase "Give the Dog a Good Name" was recommended by Dale Carnegie, and means that part of being clear is saying what really needs to be said. In other words, when you communicate, the words you use matter—because different words communicate different things.

Specifically, if you are a leader, be sure you say the truly important things over and over. Repeat the things that truly need to be heard.

It's surprising how many people fail to do this. Many of us communicate by trying to say things we think the listener will like or understand, rather than clearly saying the most important things that need to be said. Or we just get caught up in our own script instead of saying what should be said.

For example, an old story from sales training seminars is told of the salesman who unexpectedly finds himself on the elevator with the CEO of a company he's visiting. The CEO notices him, and in a friendly voice asks him what he's doing there that day.

The salesman, a bit surprised but very excited at this development, answers: "I'm here to sell. I'm a salesman. I'm so glad to meet you." Then the elevator door opens, the CEO says "Nice to meet you, too. Good luck," and walks away. The door closes, and the salesman shakes his head in shock.

He knows he blew it. By doing what, though? Answer: He wasn't clear. He said things, and the things he said were clearly understood by the person listening. But they weren't actually clear because they didn't communicate what the salesman should have communicated.

A Better Name for the Dog

He could have responded, "My name is Alex Smithson, and I'm here to help you save 23 percent on your annual IT expenses, with an upgrade in processing speed, data security, and service. Would you like that?"

Or depending on the details, he could have said a number of things. But he needed to say something that clearly mattered. Too many people miss this when communicating.

If you are a leader or want to be, never miss an opportunity to clearly say the truly important thing about your work, company, and goals.

Another example is very telling. A number of huge companies in past decades created major business conglomerates, including Xerox and General Electric (GE).[5] Xerox poured a great deal of money into various technological projects in order to seek increased leadership in the overall tech field. But the message it emphasized — leadership in photocopying machines — was so effective that the company found it very difficult to break into other markets.

Be clear in how you communicate things. And clearly communicate the truly important things.

When potential buyers heard the name "Xerox", they thought "copiers." This was good for Xerox when its goal was selling copiers, but it struggled to expand beyond this narrow field.

Another big company, GE, took a different approach. While

in the early days the large majority of its income came from selling lighting products and services, GE leadership emphasized a different central focus.[6] Asked in the year 2000 what GE's "core expertise" was, CEO Jeffrey Immelt did not reply, "lighting" or "technology." He certainly didn't say, "photocopiers." Instead, he replied: "We pick great people, we make them better, and we retain them."[7]

He was clear about the most important thing. And he kept it very simple.

Indeed, for some time GE leadership has been consistent and clear about this overall goal and emphasis, and the people at GE understand this. This high level of clarity has allowed the company to change right along with numerous market and technological shifts—because the central goal was building people, and the people in the company clearly knew this central goal.

Again, the reason they knew this was that their leaders communicated it clearly—and repeatedly.

Frameworking: Say the Main Thing!

If you are a leader or want to be, never miss an opportunity to clearly say the truly important thing about your work, company, and goals. Be clear in how you communicate things. And clearly communicate the truly important things.

To do this, it can be very helpful to start many communications with what Michael Kinsley called a "framework."[8] This means just openly stating your purpose, like "I think you're fascinating, and I'd like to get to know you better" or "I've studied your department's financials, and I've worked up a plan to save you 18 percent on overhead."

A framework is a clear "banner statement" or "headline" that tells everyone what's going on. The right, or wrong, framework can make a huge difference in how well you communicate. For example, consider the following two attempts to tackle a sticky family situation:

1. "Son, we need to talk about your chores."
2. "Son, we need to talk about your chores because I'd like to increase your reward for when you do an especially good job."

In most families, the second of these frameworks is more likely to elicit a positive response. Even though the second discussion may well cover penalties when the chores aren't done, the framework helps get the ball rolling on an uplifting note.

Sometimes sharing your framework is more effective after you've asked questions and listened to the other person for a while. For example, during a business discussion you may learn that the other person hates his job. When the time is right, you might share the following framework: "I'm here to meet with you because I love my job. I absolutely *love* it. And I think I might be able to help you have the same experience."

Frameworking takes much of the guesswork out of communication, and it clarifies what you're doing and why. It gets rid of the big question a lot of people are silently asking themselves in many communications: "Who on earth is this guy, and why do I care?"

Of course, like all effective communication, your frameworks need to be genuine, honest, and realistic.

RULE #8

BE HONEST

"Half the world is composed of people...who have nothing to say and keep on saying it."
—ROBERT FROST

Honestly, Honesty!

Our next "big picture" principle is honesty. Put simply, it is *Rule #8: Make Your Communication Honest.*

And to be perfectly honest, we could spend an entire book on this one thing. Honesty matters deeply in communication. People need to be able to trust you. People need to know that you're an honest person and that the things you say to them are true.

Again: Communication had better be honest! If people can't trust what you say, you're going to have a very hard time communicating throughout your life.

We've all heard the story of the boy who cried wolf, and situations like this happen far too often in family, business, and

Let's be clear, it's much easier just to be honest.

other aspects of life. Most people know *that one person* in their life who lies constantly just for convenience, that one person they never know whether to believe or not.

Don't Be That Guy

It's hard to trust such a person. Chris Brady reminds us of an old saying that goes, "If you're dumb, you better be tough." Well, likewise, "If you're a liar, you better have a very good memory," because you're going to spend your whole life trying to cover for what you covered all those times you covered.

Let's be clear, it's much easier just to be honest. And it's the right thing to do. Honesty is the most effective and best way to communicate.

Note that a lot of honesty is a simple matter of consistency. You shouldn't change character on people every time you communicate. Be yourself, the same, genuine self.

Your Primary Communication

At home and in your professional life, people need to know that you have integrity and that you mean what you say. They need to know what you represent, that you're on message, that you "walk the talk," and that you're consistent. They also need to know that your word is your bond. When you say something, they need to be

Honesty is the most effective and best way to communicate.

able to fully trust it. Without this, they can never see you as a leader.

They won't follow, and you'll have nobody to lead.

In short, your honesty, or lack of it, is perhaps the most important communication you share with people.

Be honest.

RULE #9

COMMUNICATE OFTEN

"We are happiest making others happy."
—CHRIS BRADY

Noticing People

Our next "Big Picture" guideline is that *The Best Communicators Communicate Often.*

Most people tend to have the tightest bonds and the deepest relationships with those who are closest to them. Of course, there are people we rub shoulders with that we may not feel particularly close to, but it's difficult to feel really connected to a person we never spend any time around.

With that said, good communication is important to infrequent relationships as well. One of the steps to communicating is to be a communicator. Talk to people. Get to know

> **The Best Communicators Communicate Often.**

people in line at the grocery store or in the lobby of the dentist. Reach out to people, compliment, take notice, and be a communicator.

This will help you practice your communication skills, and it will help you be a better person, friend, and leader. In fact, wherever possible, communicate in ways that will make people happier—even if just for a few minutes in their day. Great communicators use communication to help and bless people.

An Amazing Day

A friend told the following story of spending an afternoon with business leader Orrin Woodward as they ran errands. He said: "It was like a hands-on workshop about making friends and building relationships. When we fueled the car, Orrin introduced himself to the gas station attendant and struck up a conversation about his work and his family. By the time the tank was full and we paid for the gas, we knew that the man was married, had two kids, hated his job, and wanted to find a better way to make a living.

"And the man knew that Orrin was married, had four kids, and loved his work. He also knew that Orrin would be calling him later to help him find a way to love his work as well. It was really amazing.

"At first, I thought it was just that one guy. Boy, was I wrong. Orrin took that kind of interest in everyone we met. We got a haircut, and no sooner did the lady start clipping than Orrin asked her if she liked her work. She said it was a decent job. He launched into how much he loves his job. Within seconds she was asking, 'What's your job?'

"Within five minutes she asked, 'Could I do your kind of job?' And by the time our haircuts were done the other people in the shop wanted to do what Orrin does as well. It was really impressive.

"Then we went to another store, and the whole thing was repeated. And later the same thing at the restaurant where we ate lunch. The whole day was meeting people, talking, learning about them, telling them about us, and making friends. It was surprising and amazing. And it was also a lot of fun."

Really Care

"One thing really stood out to me. At first I thought maybe Orrin was just using our errands as a business trip, which is a good thing. I'm not in the same business as Orrin, but I respected what I thought he was doing.

"But as I watched I realized something. If someone didn't have any interest in Orrin's business, that didn't deter him at all. He just kept getting to know the person, even if business had nothing to do with it. He was genuinely out to make friends, and he did it with everyone who crossed our path that day. He gave them support, friendship, and a smiling wink. When we left, they were all smiling their heads off.

"It made me realize that I can be a much more friendly, caring, and communicative person. More to the point, that is the kind of person we all should be. The world was a better place for me that day, because I met so many people and got to know them—people I would normally just ignore. I realized that the world can be better each day if we'll just be more communicative and friendly."

Top leaders communicate a lot. It's part of what made them top leaders and part of what continues to make them great leaders over time.

Leaders shouldn't forget that communicating often keeps things top-of-mind for people. Without frequent communication, the most important things can easily be forgotten. Also, communicating often can drive the message home. There is really no substitute for this. Repetition makes a huge difference.

Communicating often also increases the accuracy of what is understood and received. It naturally and effectively clears up or diminishes miscommunications.

Communicating often lets people know that what you are sharing must be important. And it shows that you care.

Communicating often builds confidence in people for your leadership. It invites discussion and further dialogue.

Communicating often makes people feel more "in the know" and connected. It shows transparency and openness.

Communicating often sets a pattern that others will follow.

RULE #10

YOUR WORDS WILL GIVE YOU AWAY, SO GET YOUR HEART RIGHT

*"Everything becomes a little different
as soon as it is spoken out loud."*
—HERMANN HESSE

Dead Giveaway

It is important to realize that your communication is always saying something about you.

Once you get past how you actually say things—or don't say something when you really should—it's time to remember that the words are very important too. For instance, in a work setting, do you often use the words *I*, *me*, and *myself*? Or do you usually say *we* and *us*? This one thing can be a major giveaway about how you're thinking, where your ego is, how much credit you hog versus what you give away, your leadership ability, and so on.

Almost everyone notices these things, even when they don't mean to. And a few people *actively* and *purposely* watch for such things. In fact, top leaders often listen to these very things to see who the next generation of leaders will be. And most of us have a sort of internal detector built in so that we pick things up from the communication when someone is off track.

They're Always Watching

The words you say give you away.

And not only words, but also tone, gestures, body language, eye contact, emphasis, and interestingly enough, the times you close your mouth and let others do the talking. To repeat: Your communication gives you away.

It gives away your flaws a lot of the time, but it also gives away your strengths—the things you really care about, and your core character. And, eventually, your communication gives away your real goals.

What you plan to communicate will frequently be overshadowed by your real motivations, emotions, and goals.

For example, is a great teacher really a great teacher if the student never learns? Is a great speaker really a great speaker if his audience doesn't change? Communication isn't just speaking or making a point—it's being heard and, understood and making a difference in the minds and hearts of those you're communicating with.

To change lives, in the words of bestselling author Oliver DeMille, effective communication can't just be *informational*, it has to be *transformational*. What you say and how you say it will give away what you really want to transform. If your goal is just to make money for yourself, or get the next promotion, that's going to come through in your communication. But if you really care about people, and want to help them, that will come through instead.

The Heart of Communication

Given all this, it's important to get your heart right, because what you plan to communicate will frequently be overshadowed by your real motivations, emotions, and goals. Sometimes people get confused and think this applies only to verbal communication; but even in written form, if you want to communicate a message, you have to say it a certain way—and it has to come from a genuine place of truth.

> **Communication isn't just speaking or making a point— it's being heard and, understood and making a difference in the minds and hearts of those you're communicating with.**

How you format things, the order of the words, punctuation, and so on, changes the meaning, and sometimes the feeling, of your writing. But most importantly, when you are speaking to or with people, how you really feel about things—and about the people you're talking to— will come through.

If you're off (even if you try to hide it), it's eventually going to show.

The Biggest of All

So get your heart right. This is a key element of effective communication. And, indeed, when your heart is truly right, most people will see that and look past the little mistakes or errors you make. It's best to get both things right—your heart and your words—but the heart is the most important. This is a truly "Big Thing" when you want to be an effective communicator.

In reality, it is often the biggest thing of all.

PART THREE

THE QUICK FIXES
(Sometimes Called the "Little Things")

"The most important thing in communication
is hearing what isn't said."
—PETER DRUCKER

LEADERS REMEMBER NAMES

"Don't you forget about me...."
—THE BREAKFAST CLUB

The Little Things

We've already discussed four of the most basic rules of communication in Part One, and in Part Two we talked about some of the "Big Things" that make your communication sink or swim. Now we'll address some of the "little things" that can make or break your communication, leadership, and goals.

Don't let the fact that we're calling them "little" fool you. They make a world of difference. They're only "little" because many people think they're not all that important, but such a view is just plain wrong. Top leaders know that these little things are really just more big things.

As you read this section, we encourage you to start right now by applying the "little things." In fact, these are also known as "quick fixes" because it's relatively simple to immediately incorporate them into your communications. That makes this section especially helpful right away.

What's in a Name?

So what exactly are these "little things" or "quick fixes"? Let's start with *Rule #11: Leaders Remember Names.* Skip this, and your other communication techniques won't do nearly as much good. For example:

"Hey, Johnny…uh, Bob…I mean Mark… Wait, what was your name again? Oh, great, Tom. Now I remember. Anyway, I have a fantastic message for you tonight. I've been thinking about you ever since our last meeting, and I have some great ideas to share that I think you'll really connect with."

Really? If you've been thinking so much about helping me, how did you forget my name?

Not a very good start. In fact, wherever else this meeting goes, the communication began pretty badly. On the other hand, what if your meeting went more like this:

"Hey, Tom, it's so good to see you again! I've been thinking about our last meeting a lot, and I have some really good ideas to share with you that I think you'll like."

Wow! He remembered my name!

Top leaders know that remembering names is an important skill to develop, and effective communicators take the time to do it.

We could say a lot about this point, but it's straightforward and simple. Remember the names of people you meet.

This is basic and very important. If you want people to care what you say, you need to show them you care enough to at least remember who they are. This powerful "little thing" can make a huge difference.

Train Yourself

But let's take this a step further. If you want to be a top leader, you can't just say, "I'm not good at remembering names," and excuse yourself from ever having to try. If you are committed to being an excellent communicator, you have to do whatever it takes to get good at remembering names.

Fortunately, Chris Brady shared a couple of very helpful tips on remembering names. First, he taught that top leaders know that remembering names is an important skill to develop, and effective communicators take the time to do it. This is the place to start, by realizing how important it is.

Second, he asked, "Why are so many of us so bad at this? It should be basic, right?" One of the main reasons lots of people struggle to remember names is that, in Brady's words, "They're too busy thinking about themselves in a social setting to focus on someone else for a second."

That's sad. The way he said it is also very significant. "Too busy…to focus…for a second." Just one second could actually make quite a difference.

Just one second.

SIDEBAR TO READER:

Think about it. ONE second is about the time it takes to look in the mirror, or put on your sock. You might want to look at your reflection for a longer period of time, but just one second will give you a pretty good assurance that it's actually you staring back in that mirror.

A single second is way less than how long it takes to tweeze an errant eyebrow. Or, if you're the kind of guy who has never tweezed your eyebrows or asked a barber to help you in this little chore, it's less time than it takes to move your eyebrows out of the way when you want to see something really important.

Just one second. Seriously.

The Four-Second Revolution

Or, even better, how about four seconds?

You can do a lot in four seconds. More on this below. But first, here are several excellent tips that Brady shared on how to more easily remember names. If you're not good at this skill, slow down, take notes, make a plan, and incorporate these recommendations into your daily interactions.

Make no mistake. Remembering names is a very, very important communication skill. Brady recommended:

1. Always be the first to introduce yourself. This allows you to be in control, and you know what's coming. Otherwise the person mentions his or her name and quickly moves on to other topics before

you were really prepared to listen. You hadn't yet turned on your "I'm Going To Remember His Name" button.

But if you take the initiative, you've got a little warning to yourself, so you can really pay attention when he says his name. You're ready, because you're leading out.

2. If you don't hear the person's name the first time, ask her to repeat it. You might think this will bother her, but in fact, most people love it when others care enough to really listen, and most people kind of like the sound of their own name. Having her repeat it isn't a bad plan at all. It means you've heard it more than once, even though it didn't quite register the first time.

    This will pay off later when you see her at the grocery store and can say hello to her by name.

3. If the person's name is a little strange, have him repeat it so you get the correct pronunciation. "Wait, you said your name is…okay, thanks. Carl. I've got it this time." Now, the name Carl probably won't be all that difficult to pronounce. But what if his name is Des Moines? If you have any doubt about pronunciation, ask.

4. Repetition is powerful. It's helpful to repeat her name aloud, to say it once or twice, associating her name to her face. "Your name is Jenny? Hi, Jenny, nice to meet you." This little tidbit can make a huge difference for your memory.

By the way, repetition also helps improve your communications in other ways because repeating important ideas, principles, and statistics can help the people you communicate with remember these things. This happens when people repeat false information as well,[9] so be sure to get your story straight—and then repetition helps you make your main points.

Here's another key that can help you remember someone's name:

5. When you learn someone's name, learn a fact about her that will help you remember. This not only makes you a better communicator, it makes you more likeable and fun. When you see her later, you can say, "Hi, Jane, how is your son's baseball team doing?"

    It might seem like this is even more difficult, because now you have to remember two things—a name and a fact. But in reality the fact usually helps you remember the name, and vice versa.

And, Repeat...

Top leaders know that remembering names is a skill worth working for and really developing. These five little "memory morsels" can greatly help. Now, to show just how powerful repetition can be, we're going to repeat these five items. Unless you have an amazing memory, you probably didn't quickly memorize them all the first time through.

Really try to remember them each as we repeat them this time:

1. Turn on your "I'm Going to Remember His Name" button as soon as you meet someone. One of the best ways to do this is to take the initiative and introduce yourself first.

2. If you don't hear his name the first time, ask him to repeat it. Even if you immediately forget it during the initial conversation, hearing him repeat it will help. Repetition makes a positive difference.

3. Make sure you know how to pronounce his name correctly. Actually, sometimes it's even easier to remember a name that's a tad hard to pronounce — but only if you're paying attention and trying.

4. If possible, repeat the person's name aloud a few times during your conversation.

5. When it's practical, also learn one fact about the person. The fact will help you remember his name, and his name will help you remember the fact. This kind of memory synergy can be very effective.

Back to Four Seconds

Now, as promised, let's talk more about the Four-Second Revolution. Note that your part in implementing the tips outlined

Don't forget what four seconds of real care and focus can accomplish.

above is only going to take about four seconds. You really listen when he shares his name, you make sure you heard it, you get the pronunciation right, and you repeat his name several times (and even more times silently in your head).

Each little piece of this usually takes only a second or two of your time, and together they amount to around four seconds—or only a bit more. Then perhaps you spend four more seconds learning a fact about him.

Regardless of the timing—whether this takes you four seconds or twenty seconds or more—going the extra mile to learn the names of people you meet will greatly increase your communication skill.

Big Connections

Again, you can mess up a lot of things with those you communicate with, but if you see them months later and say, "Hey, Des Moines, how are you? It's been a long time!", the very fact that you remember his (or her) name will mean a lot. And if you add a question about the community theater Shakespeare play he was memorizing lines for when you met him, you've made a fan for life.

If you are really thinking about the other person, and you truly give him your full attention and work to remember his name, you'll get good at this process. Don't forget what four seconds of real care and focus can accomplish. And eight seconds is even better.

This might seem little, but it's actually the opposite.

Top leaders remember names.

RULE #12

AVOID THE BIG SLIPS

"I am not a speed reader. I am a speed understander."
—Isaac Asimov

Don't Slip Up

The second "quick fix" is somewhat obvious, yet many people make a serious communication mistake by not remembering it.

Avoiding the "Big Slips" means being careful not to let that incredibly dumb thing slip out as you're communicating with others. Don't say the really wrong thing. This can mean anything from super awkward small talk when you first meet someone (like: "Hey, I'm Marcus. What did you eat for dinner? I ate broccoli. I just love broccoli. Isn't it a truly wonderful vegetable? Do you have a favorite vegetable? Is it broccoli?"), to the comments you make to people at any point in the conversation that you should just plain never say.

We're talking about comments like "Oh my goodness! When is your baby's due date?" to a woman who isn't actually pregnant....

That's bad.

Or maybe you pick up your date for the evening and the first thing you say is, "Wow, you look so tired!"

Ah! Not good. You'll want to take that one back.

Or you're on the date and respond to a question: "My greatest life achievement? Well that would have to be reaching level 90 on World of Warcraft, which is one of the most important games in the world. What about you?" Or, "Hi, Kelsey, I just love puppets. Puppets are so wonderful, don't you think? I could make a puppet of you if you'd like."[10]

Actually, there are a lot of dumb things or Big Slips you could say on a date or in a meeting—there are entire lists all over the Internet—but this goes for all other communication as well. Avoid the Big Slip.

More Thoughts

For example, it's typically not recommended to start conversations by talking about the weather. Unless, of course, the weather has been an extreme event and not mentioning it would seem strange (e.g., "Hurricane Sandy? Last week? I never noticed").

It's worth it to find the right words, rather than floundering around and stumbling on the Big Slips of the world.

George Herbert said, "Good words are worth much, and cost little." It's worth it to find the right words, rather than floundering around and stumbling on the Big Slips of the world. As the old saying goes, "If you don't have anything good to say, don't say anything at all." While this was originally about avoiding gossip or criticizing others, it can also apply in many kinds of communication. Really, silence is nearly always better than saying negative things that unwittingly offend or hurt.

Obviously, it would take too long to list every potentially wrong thing it is possible to say, but the point is that you should probably think about what you say before you open your mouth. A few things are simply off limits, like commenting on the person's physique in any way that is too forward or awkward, criticizing or gossiping in any way, or even complimenting things that are none of your business or patently private (e.g., "Wow! You're so beautiful. I had no idea my meeting would be with someone so gorgeous. Are you married? Man, you're beautiful"). This comes across as creepy. And wrong.

Avoid the Big Slip.

How to (Try to) Recover

But what if you don't? After all, a Big Slip is a *slip*. It's not like you planned it. Sometimes you blow it, and if this happens, immediately call it for what it is. This is almost the only effective way to recover from a big slip.

It takes humility. And you have to do it immediately. No stalling. No hoping it will all go away. Just jump in and fix it by calling yourself out and apologizing.

> "Hi. Nice to meet you. When is your baby due?"
>
> "I'm not pregnant."
>
> "Oh my gosh. I'm sorry. I can't believe I just said that. Wow! That was so unprofessional. I am so sorry."

It's okay to lay it on a bit thick. But you have to be genuine and sincere as you say these things.

Clearly, it's much better to simply avoid the Big Slip. If you don't, do your best to immediately call yourself out, apologize, and then call yourself out some more. Then stop, as soon as the person forgives you.

In short: Avoid the Big Slip.

(This applies to face-to-face conversation. It should go without saying that if you make such a slip in writing or online, it's probably not as much of a "slip." Always think before you hit "send"!)

RULE #13

USE COMMUNICATION SOFTENERS

"Communication is everyone's panacea for everything."
—TOM PETERS

Extremely Misunderstood

A third "quick fix" is easy: add a few well-considered extra words here and there to soften your language. This can really improve your communication.

Now don't get us wrong. We understand the power of being bold, and many times the best choice is to say a thing straight out without beating around the bush. But using communication softeners sometimes can help you communicate more effectively.

As a general rule, it's good not to offend people with nuances or extreme language before even getting to the point of your message. You probably don't want someone to stop listening to you — or write you off as rude or extreme — before you even have a chance to share your main point.

> **Softening your language can make a big difference. Just relax and watch yourself as you speak to others.**

Using communication softeners is a way to make your language less offensive and more understanding of others. Again, if you offend your audience (big or small) before they ever hear your message, you're probably doing something wrong.

(Notice we didn't say, "You *are* doing something wrong." We said "probably," which is a communication softener. Saying "you are" is far too universal in this case, and you'll find that many people will argue with you about such words, rather than hearing your actual point.)

It's Simple

This is a truly *quick* fix if you add a few extra words to soften your tone here and there. The positive impact on your communication will usually be quite significant. Here are a few examples:

"I could be wrong, but—"

"Perhaps we could try—"

"Maybe I heard you wrong, but did you say—?"

Even adding a *probably*, a *perhaps*, or a *maybe* often makes a big difference. Of course, as we just showed, words like *often* can also soften meanings in a conversation.

Softening your language can make a big difference. Just relax and watch yourself as you speak to others. Try to be less rigid in your words and a little more understanding. Doing so will have a great impact on your communication in almost all settings—especially with those who are closest to you (or people you are meeting for the first time).

Instead of:

"I totally disagree…"

Try:

"I'm not sure I understand you clearly. Did you mean to say that…"

Or instead of:

"You'll always be a failure unless…"
"The way to do this is…"
"Well, the president said that I'm right because…"

Try adding communication softeners:

"Many people have failed because they didn't…"
"In my experience, the best way to do this is…"
"You know, the president said something about this that might be helpful…"

As mentioned, there is certainly a time and a place to be bold and direct and to leave out any such communication softeners. But this usually doesn't occur at the beginning of your relationship or at the start of a conversation, speech, or other communication.

Nor is it usually the best approach during a conflict or when emotions are running high. As Proverbs 15:1 teaches: "A gentle answer turns away wrath, but a harsh word stirs up anger." Or in another translation: "A soft answer turneth away wrath...."

Communication softeners can greatly improve communication, leadership, and overall effectiveness.

Conclusion

If you apply these three "quick fixes" as outlined in Part Three (remember names, avoid big slips, use communication softeners), you'll frequently be amazed at the new level of communication you'll attain. Likewise, the people you're able to help will appreciate your happier, more inspiring tone.

By applying these three "little" rules right away, you'll begin witnessing huge growth in your power to communicate effectively.

PART FOUR

LISTEN UP!

"I like to listen. I have learned a great deal from listening carefully. Most people never listen."
—ERNEST HEMINGWAY

BE AN ACTIVE *LISTENER*

"Words are, of course, the most powerful drug used by mankind."
—RUDYARD KIPLING

First, Middle, and Last: Connect!

The great Dale Carnegie famously taught that "the big secret of dealing with people" is simply to connect with the individual. If you do this consistently and effectively, you'll be a much better leader than if you fall short in this vitally important responsibility.

But that's not all. Really connecting means really *connecting*. And the next step in this is very important:

> To really *connect* with the individual, learn to truly *listen!*

Just Listen

The habit of listening can be hard for many people to adopt, but it is also essential for effective communication. People often believe that communication consists merely of getting your point across, and at one level, they're right. But communication can and should be much more.

In fact, much can be communicated without any words at all. As Marcel Marceau said, "To communicate through silence is a link between the thoughts of man." In reality, communication is a link between people's thoughts, and oftentimes the best way to arrive at such a connection is using silence. Other times words are most effective. And believe it or not, the highest level of communication frequently comes by truly listening while the other person speaks.

Because communication is a link, it requires work on both sides. It's not just one person blabbering away to the other. It's the link they share. Otherwise, it's not really communication. That's not to say that if both people don't have a chance to speak, nothing was communicated. An orator delivering a speech to an auditorium of thousands can still be a very effective communicator and can make a difference in many lives—as long as both sides of the link are open and ready to learn.

On the other hand, if you think you can get away with always speaking and never listening, and still be an effective communicator, you will no doubt find that your communication falls short in many circumstances. There is certainly a time when you should speak, but listening is just as important—and often even more important.

> **All effective communication is based on mutual understanding. Without quality listening, mutual understanding is always weak.**

Energetic Energy

In most communication, there is a time to listen. *Not* just a time to hold your breath for a momentary pause while the other person takes a minute to speak his mind before you spout your point again. You must authentically *listen* if you want to grow in this area of communication.

Listening isn't always the easiest thing to do, as illustrated with the following story:

> A man turned to his friend and asked sadly, "What ever happened with you and Suzy? You were so good together! Why did it fall apart?"
>
> The other man shrugged, unsure of that answer himself. "I don't know," he admitted. "She said I wasn't a good listener or something. I wasn't exactly paying attention."

Funny. But, actually, it's not that humorous if it resembles your communication in real life. To connect with the individual, you have to pay attention. As best-selling author John Maxwell taught, connecting is about energy.

This bears repeating: *Connecting is about energy.*

For example, does your communication show that your energy is about caring? Or is it about something else? Is your energy about *you*? Or is it really about the person you're communicating with? This matters because selfish energy, even self-centered energy, isn't usually uplifting. It's sometimes downright off-putting. It shuts down

Good listeners are naturally better connectors, because they foster an environment of mutual understanding, mutual support, and shared goals.

the interpersonal connection that is the basis of trust, genuine sharing, and true communication.

All effective communication—the right kind of energy in relationships and other interactions—is based on mutual understanding. Without quality listening, mutual understanding is always weak.

Listen for Plot

In addition to other kinds of listening, it can help to remember that most people have a recognizable communication Plot or Plotline. This means they are communicating with you, or listening to communication from you, for an important reason. They're not just passing time. There is a purpose to their participation in the communication process.

Knowing their purpose—their communication Plotline (what some might call an agenda)—can greatly help you understand them and respond to them in ways they'll most effectively understand. Consider the following major communication Plotlines:

- **Passion.** Some people are doing what they do because they love it, or they deeply believe in it. When you communicate with such people, show appreciation for what they might be passionate about.

    You're not really listening to Passion people if you don't notice that passion is a central driving force for them. Learn what they are passionate about and what words and ideas most effectively motivate them, and then incorporate such insights into your communication as you work with them.

- **Empowerment.** In contrast, some people are motivated mainly by helping others, by serving people and seeing them learn, grow, improve, and succeed.

  > **When you connect with the other person, real communication is both possible and probable.**

  Don't focus your communication with such people on things that are directly about the ones you are talking to. Instead, focus on how they can help others—the people they serve and care about. Empowerment people don't talk as much about goals, achievements, or even ideas as they do about other people, people they really want to help. Noticing this as you listen allows you to more effectively understand and communicate with them.

- **Challenge.** Still other people are truly excited only when they face challenges and have to do amazing things to achieve a goal. For such people, the bigger the challenge, the greater their enthusiasm.

  Improve your communication with Challenge people by sharing stories of other people who have given their *all* to some big, incredible challenge—and kept going until they won. Also be encouraging about the challenges or obstacles the Challenge person is encountering. Cheer them on.

- **Stories.** Some people really like a good story, an engaging movie, online vine, video, discussion, etc. They love to hear interesting and enjoyable experiences, facts, or fun tales, and they like to share them with anyone who will listen. Storytellers are easy to spot, because they tell you stories. Or if they just heard you speak, for example, they approach you and comment—not on your speech, message, or ideas but on a story you told or the cool online video you mentioned.

  To communicate more effectively with Storytellers...you guessed it... tell motivating stories. And since stories are often the quickest way to connect with Passion, Empowerment, and Challenge types as well, work important stories into your communication.

  > **Becoming a better storyteller will help you in most arenas where communication is needed.**

  Moreover, learn to tell effective stories frequently, in the right way, and with the use of enthusiasm. Becoming a better storyteller will help you in most arenas where communication is needed.

- **Structure.** Finally, some of the people you'll communicate with in life and work do best when your communication is part of an easy or catchy structure. Structuralists thrive when you share things like *The 7 Habits, The 4 Essentials of Leadership, The Color Code, The Five Laws of Decline, SPLASH Public Speaking, Rascals vs. Everyone Else, The 8 F's of Living Intentionally For*

Excellence, etc. Give them a list, a model, or a picture in their head, and they'll really get what you're trying to communicate.

Add a dash of humor to any or all of these types of communication, and you'll be a more effective communicator—whoever you're speaking, writing, texting, or listening to. Top leaders learn to incorporate all five of these types of communication (plus a bit of humor) into most or all of their interactions.

Again, connection is necessary for real communication, and thinking about the different ways to connect with people can help you boost the quality of your communications to increasingly effective levels. As you listen to people, note which of these plotlines they bring up.

Listen for Individuality

Of course, if you spend too much time trying to figure out the other person's communication Plotline, personality style, etc., you'll find that you're not a very good listener. To *really* listen, you must also put aside preconceptions and truly focus on the other person. What does he want?

> **Good listeners validate the individual and genuinely seek to connect.**

What is she really seeking? What does he want you to know? What's her real purpose right now as she talks with you (or e-mails, posts, etc.)?

Good listeners validate the individual, and genuinely seek to connect. With that said, listening for the other person's communication Plotline can also be very helpful.

As you may have noticed by now, working to improve as a leader requires being a better communicator, and as you increase your communication skills you'll nearly always boost many leadership traits. Those who develop the skills of good listening are naturally, and simultaneously, developing their leadership abilities. Good leaders are good listeners, and great leaders are great listeners.

RULE #15

BE AN ACTIVE LISTENER

"Those who serve, deserve."
—ORRIN WOODWARD

Active, not Passive

To be an active, rather than a passive, listener, it is important to be truly engaged in what the other person is trying to communicate. You're listening. You're letting it come in. You're trying to really connect with the other person, to hear him, to absorb what he's saying. To genuinely *understand* him.

In the excellent book *Personality Plus* by Florence Littauer, we learn that listening is much more difficult for some personalities and people than others. For the

Choleric personality type (driver), listening can very often seem like a waste of time. (e.g. "What could the other person have to say that could possibly be more important than what I'm trying to tell her?")

People with the Sanguine personality (excited/ outgoing) might not even think about listening, because they're usually so focused on their own agenda that it simply never crosses their mind to slow down, focus, and attentively listen to what the other person has to say.

On the other hand, listening tends to come much easier to the Phlegmatic and Melancholic personalities. Phlegmatic (peaceful/relaxed) individuals often really love to listen to others — usually more than they like talking themselves.

And lastly, though the Melancholic personality (intro-verted/meticulous) might prefer being alone altogether, because he tends to desire silence and deep thinking over any speaking at all, when he is around other people he usually prefers listening to speaking. But he also needs to focus on listening, not just zoning off and thinking about something else.

Knowing your personality type, even from something as simple as this list above, can help you consider whether listening is one of your strengths or weaknesses. It's helpful to take stock of this. If you aren't a good listener, this chapter (and the previous one) are extremely important for you.

Skill, not Talent

But let's be clear: though some people have a more difficult time listening actively, they can still learn to do it. And to be leaders, we must all do this.

Like remembering names, great listening is a *skill* rather than a *talent*. As one leader put it: "Talent is something you have. Skills are something you have to develop. And talent is simply not enough."

Or as actor Will Smith said: "Talent is a gift. Skill comes from hard work."

Talent is not enough. We need to develop skills that increase the influence and impact of our communication.

Again, leadership-level listening is a very important skill. If you develop it, no matter what personality traits you were born with, you will see a huge shift in the effectiveness of your communication. If not, your leadership will suffer.

Stand Up and Dance

Moreover, as this chapter's heading suggests, it is necessary to put the "active" into active listening. This means that you seriously and attentively put your whole energy into opening up and receiving what the other person is trying to share.

Communication is the spark of all success, all progress, and all improvement.

This is crucial to quality communication. No writer can ultimately communicate better than her readers are willing to openly receive.

No speaker can communicate more effectively than his listeners choose to accept. No conversation between two people can be better than the weakest member agrees to allow.

Communication is always at least two-sided. If one side closes down, the communication isn't very good. And the listener often has most of the power. A writer can create the best novel or leadership book in the world — but its ultimate influence will depend on those reading it, those on the listening end of the communication. The same is true in a speech, meeting, letter, or electronic interaction.

Speaking is just speaking, and writing is just writing, without a truly active listener. But add an enthusiastic, attentive listener to the mix, and the result can sometimes be a bit of a miracle: communication.

Footprints in the Sand!

This point has been made many times before, but imagine how Robison Crusoe must have felt after a long time stranded on a deserted island, when suddenly he came across something that changed his whole world: the footprint of another man in the sand. It was a moment of shock, fear, and hope all rolled into one. And it was a moment of potential.

The potential, ultimately, was the simple possibility of communication and, through communication, a deeper and better connection and everything that could come from that (including being rescued). For Crusoe, this was a true miracle.

Eye contact is vital in communication. Even a speaker who presents a message to a large audience can use eye contact to truly make or break the effectiveness of his message.

For example, there may be one person in the room who's thinking: "Wow, this is really great!" But if the speaker makes meaningful eye contact with him, the message can drive even more deeply home. You may have been that audience member before, and though you probably shouldn't choose whether to learn from a speaker based on whether he looks at you among the hundreds or thousands in the room, when you are the speaker, you might try to look the room over and give every section of the audience a few seconds of your visual attention.

This really does make a difference. Many speakers have found eye contact to be a very powerful tool in communication, and it matters even more for one-on-one conversations.

Keep It Appropriate

On the other hand, Chris Brady suggests you not be *too* enthusiastic with your eye contact. Don't go overboard. Don't freak people out with it. It's fine to blink once in a while or even look down at your hands for a moment while considering what the other person is saying. If you learn to use eye contact well, you might find that some of the most powerful moments are those when you break that eye contact for a moment, even while you're hearing the other person speak.

By the way, this is also important when you are speaking with someone and your smart- phone rings or vibrates. It is tempting to look away and turn your attention to the phone, but this can come across as very rude. It's especially rude when you repeatedly break eye contact in order to keep checking your phone.

> **Many speakers have found eye contact to be a very powerful tool in communication, and it matters even more for one-on- one conversations.**

The first step is to pay atten- tion to that person. Use eye contact in a moderate but truly attentive way, and then learn when the right times may be to break that eye contact briefly.

Just Do It

It's probably not necessary to say a lot about this rule. But don't just ignore it. Good eye contact is a very important part of effective communication in many settings. Use it. Pay attention to it. If you're looking away a lot, you're actually communicating something you probably don't want (e.g., you're tired, inattentive, shifty, distracted, weird, etc.).

Look people in the eye. And do it naturally, not like you're doing it just because you know you're supposed to.

RULE #17

SUMMARIZING IS VERY HELPFUL

*"Extremists think 'communication' is
agreeing with them."*
—Leo Rosten

The Summary in Your Listen

A top leader must learn to change things up as he listens and also as he speaks, writes, or communicates in other ways. At times, it helps to use brief summaries to ensure that you're on the same page with the other person.

Indeed, people sometimes don't realize (or they forget) that part of listening is summarizing. For example, when you've really given your full attention and listened to what the other person has to say and how she feels, don't just stand there. Don't just turn and walk away. And don't just grin. Naturally, and with the same seriousness you had as you listened, briefly summarize the other person's main point. Then ask, "Am I getting this right?" or "Am I understanding you correctly?" or "So what you're saying is…."

This is actually quite easy. Summarizing is really just repeating what the other person said but in your own words.

Round Two

Let's try another example. The other person takes five minutes to tell you his point, and you listen attentively, nod occasionally, and use effective eye contact to signal that you're still interested. When he gets to a break, or waits for you to affirm his words, take a few seconds to sum them up: "What I'm understanding is that you're really excited for this new opportunity and that it's everything you've been hoping for." Or "So basically, you're feeling a little misled because you gave it your all, and she didn't even try to understand you. Is that kind of how you're feeling?"

This may seem strange to some people, but a simple, short summary of the other person's words can have a huge impact on the communication because it helps him feel heard. It also allows him to gauge how well (or poorly) he's communicated, and he can amend your summary if needed in order to be more clear. This kind of interaction is basic, but it is worth discussing because it is truly essential.

Of course, after you've given your full attention, held eye contact, and really heard what he had to say, it may be your turn to talk again. And you probably have things you want to say at this point. But before you move to your own thoughts, it is a powerful communication method to take a few moments first and summarize what the other had to say.

As basic and simple as this is, most people don't do it. They get focused on what they want to say, and they simply skip the summary. But skipping the summary often communicates to the other person that you weren't really listening. This is why top leaders include the summary in most conversations.

Note that in a ten or fifteen minute discussion you'll likely want to summarize the other person's points three or four times — when natural breaks occur. If you get good at this, you'll be a good listener. If not, you probably won't.

The good news is that if you're going to focus on just one thing to make yourself a better communicator, this one can really upgrade your communication skills. To summarize well, you have to really listen.

"Yep Slap"

Of course, just like with eye contact, you can take this too far. If you interrupt him in the middle of his sentence and try to summarize every three words that come out of his mouth, you'll very often misunderstand him completely, and at the very least, you'll probably cause him some frustration.

Chris Brady suggests that we also avoid "yep slapping" people. Like other kinds of slaps, it can really hurt your communication.

SIDEBAR TO READER:

Is anybody picturing The Three Stooges right now?

That's some serious slapping.

But about you:

So you suddenly find yourself in another movie studio, and everyone is getting ready to film. They turn to you and tell you that you're a stuntman and you're here to film an episode of The Three Stooges.

Another stuntman walks up and stands next to you.

The director tells you both: "One of you gets to do the slapping, and the other one gets to be slapped. The two of you decide who does what."

What do you do?

The moral of this little story is that sometimes, if you want your communication to really work out well, you better talk fast!

But what exactly is a "yep slap" or a "yes slap"? You may have had this happen to you before. You're talking to someone, and every other word, he says, "Yep, yep, yep. Uhuh. Yeah, yep, yep, yep, right." Without fail. With all those *yeps*, he must be agreeing with you, or at least understanding you, right?

Actually, no. A lot of people use "yes slapping" to avoid listening and spend that time thinking about something else altogether. For example, the famous Socratic Method is based on asking lots of questions and on getting the other person thinking more deeply by the profound and challenging questions you ask.

But read the original dialogues of Plato, where the discussions of Socrates are recounted, and far too many of the people Socrates was talking to simply "yep slap" whatever he says.

They say "Yes, Socrates," "You are right, Socrates," and "That's correct, Socrates," over and over. But then, when he gets to his main point, they stop agreeing and start arguing with him. Their "yes, yes, yes" didn't mean anything, really.

The best listeners in Plato's dialogues don't do this. They let Socrates make his point, and they listen carefully, without a constant chorus of "yes, yeah, yep." At a natural gap in the conversation, they summarize what he said to be sure they understand. Then, when it's time to really discuss an important point, they understand what Socrates has said because they really listened, and they can weigh in with their own views.

To repeat: those who overuse "yes slapping" probably aren't really listening. As the person speaking to them, you may think they are with you—after all, they keep agreeing. But then you get to the end of your point and ask them, "So do you want to do it?" And of course, the natural response, since they really weren't listening all that much, must be: "Nope." You can see why this would be a problem.

In short, summarizing can be very helpful, but don't overdo it or turn it into "yep slapping."

SIDEBAR TO READER:

To help remember not to "yep slap" people, don't forget to picture The Three Stooges, like we did above.

You're probably laughing already, right? Unless you don't like their slapstick humor. But this will work either way. Picture a series of clips of The Three Stooges slapping each other.

They're slapping, slapping...more slapping.

Then picture yourself doing this kind of slapping in your business life. Not good. This doesn't win friends and positively influence people. Dale Carnegie wouldn't approve.

Now, picture yourself not slapping people.

Good! That's much better.

Finally, picture yourself not "yes slapping" them either.

In short, summarize. It forces you to really listen, and it is a respectful way to show the other person that you are one of those rare people who is actually focused on what he is saying. Doing this one thing will bring significant improvement to your communication and leadership.

RULE #18

DON'T INTERRUPT

*"A leader is always first in line during times of criticism
and last in line during times of recognition."*
—ORRIN WOODWARD

Let Them Talk

Let's just take a few seconds and add one more key rule.

In addition to not "yes slapping," it's also important not to continually interrupt other people with too many words, arguments, or questions. This is vital. The main part of listening is keeping your mouth shut for a time and letting the other person get her point across. If you keep interrupting her as she's trying to speak, you may unwittingly be telling her that you think your words are worth more than hers and that you don't really care what she has to say.

Obviously this isn't what most of us are trying to communicate. On the other hand, some people with a Choleric personality (driver) may actually think this way in certain situations, which is not necessarily a good thing for their communication. But many of us get this wrong at times, whatever our personality style.

We may even think that interrupting to agree or to add something to the speaker's point proves that we're really on her side, and there is definitely a time for that. But usually it's better to let her talk and to wait until she's done before trying to summarize her words or emphasize your own point.

Call to Order

The order here matters. As Covey put it, we should *first* seek to understand the other person and only then seek to be understood. If we really listen, we'll know better what will truly help when it's our turn to speak. This is central in effective communication.

> **The main part of listening is keeping your mouth shut for a time and letting the other person get her point across.**

Again, this rule doesn't require a lot of commentary. But it is extremely important, and top leaders live it. They apply it and keep improving themselves by consistently putting down their own ego long enough to let other people talk— while attentively, and carefully, listening.

Those who never develop this skill seldom become top leaders.

RULE #19

NOD AND ACKNOWLEDGE

"Trust is the glue of life."
—STEPHEN COVEY

The Nod

Another of Brady's suggestions is the simple tip that makes up *Rule # 19: Nod and Acknowledge.*

Again, this is so basic that it should really go without saying. However, most people don't use it nearly as often as they should. These rules of communication are very powerful and very effective, but sometimes we must remind ourselves to actually apply them.

Nodding and acknowledging the other person's words are crucial elements of genuine listening. A nod is very different from speaking aloud and saying "yes, yes." It doesn't interrupt, it communicates support, and it shows the other person you're really hearing what he's saying and not thinking about something else entirely.

Nodding attentively while the other person speaks shows that you're truly interested and engaged in his words and even that you care what he has to say. But just as with all these tips, it's important to not overdo it. "Don't become a bobblehead," as Brady put it. Don't be so overdramatic with your acknowledgments that the other person no longer even cares to get his point across but just finds himself hoping that you'll stop being strange.

Shake and Nod

In the right conversation, a puzzled look on your face or even shaking your head can accomplish the same thing. It shows that you're not quite getting it or that you have questions or simply disagree. This has to be used carefully, however, because it can shut the speaker down instead of allowing him to keep sharing.

But at the right time, it may be important to show confusion or skepticism that helps him know he needs to clarify his words. Again, if you overdo this, you'll likely just upset or distract him.

BONUS

DON'T FORGET!

"Two ears. One mouth. Use accordingly."
—Millions of Moms

Mastery

Please don't be fooled by how basic these principles are. Top leaders learn to master the basics and keep mastering the basics. It is excellence in the basics that made them top leaders in the first place and keeps them there.

You may also have noticed that several of these rules are really sub-points of the main theme. The real focus here is listening, and these guidelines can help you do it much more effectively.

Each of these rules is very helpful.

Real Mastery

Many great leaders have realized along their journeys that listening is a vital skill. In fact, it is one of the great messages of the original epic journeys—those of Abraham in the Bible and of Odysseus in Homer's *Odyssey*. In both stories, the hero starts out boldly but, through many experiences with various people in a number of places, learns the power of humility and comes to understand people more effectively. Such understanding only comes with listening, and it is essential to success.

By listening and listening *well*, great leaders learn a great deal about the people they lead—and about the many other people in the world. Without listening, no real communication, and no real leadership, can occur.

Actually, not many people achieve "greatness" without becoming attentive and discerning listeners. Listening is one of the first steps to learning. Whether from an audio, a seminar, a mentor or teacher, a book, or some other source, you won't learn much if you don't choose to really listen, hear, and apply what is said.

Strength or Weakness

So much of greatness depends on the skill of listening. If you are concerned that you don't naturally possess this skill, it's probably time to stop worrying and start listening. It can really be that simple. Apply the rules we've just covered. They are easy and very effective.

> **By listening and listening *well*, great leaders learn a great deal about the people they lead.**

If, on the other hand, you are quite sure you're a great listener, you may be in even bigger trouble than everyone else. Step back, slow down, and listen more. Top leaders know that quality listening is both essential and challenging. If you ever stop working hard to do it, or think you've arrived, you're in high danger of not being a good listener.

Listening isn't a habit like breathing that will just keep happening once you've done it a few times. Instead, listening well is the kind of habit—like jogging—that you can't just forget about. You have to actually focus on it and follow through, day after day. So listen up! It will make a major difference in the effectiveness of your communication.

PART FIVE

HEAL OR HARM

"Words are singularly the most powerful force available to humanity. We can choose to use this force constructively with words of encouragement, or destructively with words of despair. Words have energy and power with the ability to help, to heal, to hinder, to hurt, to harm, to humiliate and to humble."
—YAHUDA BERG

APOLOGIZE WELL

"Until he extends his circle of compassion to include all living things, man himself will not find peace."
—ALBERT SCHWEITZER

And We're Back!

We've covered a lot, haven't we? But aren't you starting to wonder again about your acting career and how that's going? With all these communication techniques and skills you're developing, you must be doing pretty well, right? Let's take a look and see.

You zoom in on a movie set. There you are….

You're playing an older married woman. You have five children. One is married; you're working on the rest. You have a nice home, good clothes, and a happy life.

You consider yourself a respectable woman, so it completely shocks you when another very opinionated woman barges into your home, calling herself a "lady" and expecting you and your household to treat her like royalty.

Of course, she does seem rather regal, so you try to treat her respectfully. But then she presumes to take your adult daughter from your house to your garden and lecture her about who she can or cannot marry!

Is she serious? Who does this woman think she is?

Playing your character rightly, you ignore the complete intrusion of privacy and property and let the woman do as she wishes. Of course, as a human being you have to wonder how this woman could be so completely bad-mannered.

Apologizing isn't always necessary, but when it is, you'd better do it if you intend for the communication to continue in an effective manner.

And after all this, she storms out of your house, furious—because, not surprisingly, your daughter has enough spunk to stand up to her. And does the intruder even once apologize? Nope. Not once.

This has got to bother you a little bit. Of course, you're not really one for apologizing or admitting mistakes either, but what kind of nerve must this woman have?

Quite a lot actually. Lady Catherine de Bourgh from *Pride and Prejudice* seems to have even more gall than your character, Mrs. Bennett.

The Weight of Words

What important communication lessons can we learn from this scene? For one, perhaps what goes around comes around. But beyond that, it might have helped the situation, at least a little bit, if Lady Catherine had at some later point come to Mrs. Bennett and explained her feelings and sincerely apologized for the way she acted.

Of course, we don't know for sure that she didn't do this. Maybe she did just that at some point in the book's fictional future. But judging from the way she ended things, it seems unlikely.

But really, isn't it true that sometimes a simple apology can make all the difference? Mrs. Bennett might not have spent the rest of her life having ill feelings

> **Communication goes two ways and so do apologies.**

toward Lady Catherine, had this woman taken a few simple minutes to say "I'm sorry."

As you've probably learned in your own life experience, apologizing is a vital part of communication. Of course, apologizing isn't always necessary, but when it is, you'd better do it if you intend for the communication to continue in an effective manner.

"Too Late To 'Pologize"

Rule #20: Apologize Well is vital for top leaders. Even for the toughest of the tough, there is a time to buckle down and say "I'm sorry." The simple fact is, we're not perfect. Sometimes we make mistakes. Sometimes we're wrong. Sometimes feelings get hurt, even when we didn't mean to cause harm, and it's our job as leaders to take responsibility for our actions and to do our best to make others feel understood, loved, and important.

When we do make mistakes that hurt others, we should take responsibility and try to make up for those wrong actions. But "apologizing well" isn't always just saying "sorry." Depending on the situation, it might take a little more than that. Here are a few suggestions that will help:

First: Apologize! Seriously, when the need arises, simply apologize. Just go do it. If an apology is necessary, a leader will take action and get it handled, no matter how hard or even awkward it may be.

On the other hand, doing it when you *should* also means not doing it when you *shouldn't*. If an apology in a certain situation means compromising something more important, then it may be right to wait on the apology. There is a time to let things settle, even if it may feel unsettling.

The first step to apologizing is knowing when to do it and when to hold back. Let's be clear, it's usually not a bad thing to say "sorry," even if it's "I'm sorry your feelings were hurt." But consider beforehand what kind of apology will be best and what is the right thing to do. Maybe even practice it beforehand a few times. Really get clear on what needs to be said and how to most effectively say it.

Part of good communication is to think it through and raise your standard of personal interaction. Emotionally pointing and grunting isn't always the best tactic; we can often do much better in our communication if we just try.

If your explanations turn into justifications, they'll get in the way of your real goal.

Second: Do it quickly. Usually when an apology is needed, it's needed sooner rather than later. In truth, this is nearly always the case. A lot of wounds have festered and relationships suffered because they weren't taken care of quickly enough.

Obviously an apology needs to be done at the right time, but top leaders don't put it off either. There is a real risk in waiting too long. And usually it would be better to apologize within seconds, minutes, or hours of the offense. Wait two days for something that should have been done in seconds, and the person might not even remember what you said! But you'll have suffered over it all that time for nothing.

Or even worse, during the time you waited to apologize the other person may have done or said something that will make the whole situation much more difficult.

Communication goes two ways, and so do apologies. But even when the other person needs to apologize, it's often at least partly your responsibility. If you can help the situation, say you're sorry.

Third: Do it humbly. This is a difficult task for some people, but as with many other aspects of communication, it is a skill to be mastered—a very, very important skill. Apologies should be humble. If you feel the need to apologize, you've probably been in the wrong, even if it was in a small matter. And being willing to accept your role in the wrong done is the first part of being humble.

If you must, tell the person your feelings, why you did what you did. But mostly, the point of apology is to say you're sorry and hopefully to gain her forgiveness. An apology is a time to accept your imperfection and ask pardon for it but mainly to help the other person find peace as well. If your explanations turn into justifications, they'll get in the way of your real goal.

Real humility is powerful. Accept responsibility for your actions, and own up to the wrong you may have done to someone else.

Fourth: Do it sincerely. This is important in all communication but especially when you're apologizing. Be sincere, be genuine, be real. For some people, it can be very hard to find sincerity in apologies. At times, we may do it simply because it seems like the right thing to do—and not because we're really all that sorry.

But if an apology is done in an insincere way, it tends to make the situation far worse. If you can't apologize for the words you said or the actions you took, why are you apologizing? If there's something to apologize for, there's a place for sincerity. If all you can say is "I'm sorry you were hurt," but it's genuine, it will be far better than apologizing for all that you did but doing it insincerely.

> **As with all communication, there is a time to talk and a time to listen.**

If you have reason to apologize, it shouldn't be too hard to find something to be sincere about. So focus on that, and your apology will likely mean a lot more to the other person.

Fifth: Give them a chance to talk. As with all communication, there is a time to talk and a time to listen. A large part of apologizing can be allowing the other person the opportunity to explain how he feels and how you may have hurt him.

Take time to listen, to really understand. Don't just give him your words of apology, and then hurry away. Give him your ear as well. So much of apologizing and truly saying you're sorry is allowing the other person to explain his feelings, and if you lend a listening ear, your communication will go much further than if you try to control the conversation and take up all the time expressing your thoughts. Let the other person talk! And listen without frustration or anger. Don't be defensive. Just listen, and then repeat your apology.

Lastly, **Sixth:** Do it effectively. Apologizing isn't so much about saying what you need to say as saying what another needs to hear. Of course, be honest and genuine. But if they don't feel your apology, you probably aren't doing it right. If you're just talking at them rather than *to* them, it's not real communication, and it's certainly not an effective apology.

Think beyond yourself when apologizing. Think of the other person and what she needs to hear to *feel* your sincere apology.

Put Them to Use

The next time an apology is needed, try these six guidelines out and see where they take you. They're very effective.

Being human means making mistakes. There will be times in your life when apologies are needed, and these six points can have a huge impact on the effectiveness of your communication as you apologize. Review them as needed, and make sure you apply them correctly.

***

NOTE: An excellent resource, which teaches more details and techniques about effective apologies and overcoming any kind of rift between you and another person, is *Conflict Resolution* by Life Leadership Essentials Series (available at lifeleadership.com).

RULE #21

DON'T EVER GOSSIP

"Words empty as the wind are best left unsaid."
—HOMER

Don't Be Mean

Don't gossip. Ever. A major part of this rule is the importance of understanding that most people really do gossip. In fact, many of them gossip a lot. But top leaders learn never to engage in this negative and destructive behavior. It is a bad habit, a vice that genuine leaders simply and patently avoid.

Gossiping is very simple to shun, but for those who have developed gossip as a habit, it can be difficult to break. Some people gossip in business, family, church, their neighborhood, online, and anywhere else they can find other gossip-hungry people to listen.

Actually, the *Pride and Prejudice* character Mrs. Bennett, whom we met earlier, was quite a gossip. We can learn a lot of what *not to do* by studying her actions and choices. Another thing we can learn from the movie scene recounted above is that it was gossip and rumor that brought Lady Catherine de Bourgh to the Bennett home in the first place. This is where "what goes around comes around" plays a big role.

Mrs. Bennett thrived on gossip. She was the kind of person who gossiped incessantly about everything and everyone. And in return, she earned a rather bad reputation, which sadly made things hard for her daughters. Her ultimate focus in life was to marry them well, but because of the reputation she made for herself, marrying them at all was quite a challenge.

SIDEBAR TO READER:

Since we're on the topic of *Pride and Prejudice*, remember the great quote from Mr. Bennett: "For what do we live, but to make sport for our neighbors, and laugh at them in our turn?"

Let's be clear, Mr. Bennett was wrong, and not that much of a leader. Don't gossip. It's not good for society or for communication either.

The Impact on Leadership

Just as communication is a category that will play a big part in how far you go in life, it will also significantly influence your reputation. If you are a gossip, spreading rumors and generally talking negatively about others, people will find it hard to believe what you say. Even your friends and family won't be likely to trust what you tell them. This can block whatever attempts you make at leadership, unless you simply stop gossiping and even stop listening to or repeating any gossip.

As we discussed above in Rule #8 about honesty, people need to be able to believe what you say. They need to be able to trust you. And if you talk to them negatively about other people, they'll always wonder what you're saying about them when you talk to others. This is why top leaders just don't gossip, and they refuse to let others share gossip with them.

If you're in the habit of gossiping already, or even if you sometimes slip into this, you need to free yourself from the bad reputation you are spreading about yourself.

Top leaders know the value of true listening, so they don't listen to gossip.

Next time you start whispering about someone, turn it positive at the very least. Find something genuinely good to say about them. Compliment them. Eventually, if you want to be a leader, you'll find that the only thing you say about people behind their backs is how pleasant and wonderful they are. And then the friend you're talking to right now will wonder happily, "What does she say about me when I'm not around? I like this girl!"

Shun gossip, and don't put up with it from others. Again, top leaders know the value of true listening, so they don't listen to gossip.

RULE #22

DON'T CRITICIZE FOR SPORT

"Brevity is the soul of wit."
—SHAKESPEARE

If She Had Only....

At first blush, this rule might sound a lot like the last rule (Don't Gossip), but it's a little bit different. And avoiding both of these bad habits is important.

There is certainly a time for criticism, but only if it's constructive and only in the right spirit, when both sides of the discussion are open and learning. If you're simply criticizing for sport, then you're missing out on a great opportunity to be a friend and a blessing in someone's life.

And let's be clear: some people seem to make a life out of

> **Top leaders focus on the good, and when there is a time for criticism, they do it the right way.**

criticizing for sport. They may even believe that criticizing for sport is fun.

But this is the opposite of leadership.

Criticizing for sport is more than gossiping, as bad as gossip is. Criticizing the wrong way goes beyond telling all the juicy details about someone else's life. It attacks someone and at times even attempts to hurt their reputation, their livelihood, or their relationships.

For example, there are some people who spend much of their time as "trolls" or "haters" in the world, who attack people online, electronically, or simply behind others' backs. Some do it because they're caught up in the bad habit of gossiping, but others truly do it for fun, or for profit. Really! People get paid for this! They may even gain followers.

But these are not the top leaders of the world. Top leaders focus on the good, and when there is a time for criticism, they do it the right way — personally, quietly, humbly, with an intention to really serve and help — and certainly never for sport.

Hurt or Heal?

As best-selling author Orrin Woodward put it, "Hurting people hurt people." Those who have been hurt by others sometimes seek to get back at the world by spreading such hurt. Some people claim to gain energy from hurting others, looking for someone to attack or criticize. Of course, this is a natural human tendency, to lash out at others the way someone did to us.

But real leaders don't seek revenge. And if you want to be a leader, you'll refrain from becoming a hater—or a hurter. Rather, you'll spend your time seeking to love people, compliment people, teach people, and help them improve their lives. If constructive, personal criticism is needed, you'll offer it humbly and in a spirit of love and genuine support.

Top leaders ask themselves this question: Are you a hurter or a healer? If you're a hurter, you can't lead. Not really. Only healers can really build people and spread goodness and leadership.

RULE #23

IF CRITICISM IS NECESSARY, DO IT WITH HONOR

"Apologizing does not always mean that you're wrong and the other person is right. It just means that you value your relationship more than your ego."
—Anonymous

The Right Way

Let's return just once more to the movie scene from *Pride and Prejudice.* Imagine if Lady Catherine had tried a different approach to criticizing Elizabeth. If she had done it with honor and a little bit of class, the whole event might have gone very differently.

Nobody involved left the meeting in a happy state. But had Lady Catherine approached it just a little bit differently, both of them might have left the meeting feeling heard and understood and even perhaps having made a friend. They could have at least respected each other, even if their disagreement remained. The right kind of criticism, and communication, would have been much more effective.

So how do we effectively communicate the right kind of constructive criticism? Here are a few helpful tips that can make all the difference in this form of communication:

One: Make sure there's not a better way. Sometimes criticism is the only way, but it can be very damaging, and if there's a better way, why not try that first?

For example, oftentimes praise is much more effective than criticism. Business leader Lisa Hawkins tells a story of how she treated her husband when he was first learning to speak in front of people. At the beginning of his speaking career, she felt there were almost a hundred things to criticize and only a couple of things to praise, but she knew, because of who her husband was and what kind of mentoring he needed, that the best thing would be to focus on those few good things.

So each week on the drive home after he finished speaking, she complimented him for all the good things. If there was only one good thing in the whole presentation, she focused heavily on that and ignored the other things he botched.

Little by little this praise lifted him. Each week he improved. Each presentation he got better. At some point, he was doing perhaps fifty things right and maybe twenty things wrong. You might think at this point she could finally stop focusing on the good things and tell him how to "shape up," but she didn't. For most of his speaking career she simply offered praise.

On the few occasions where he was repeatedly making a mistake that needed to be corrected, she found a way to couch that criticism in praise. "You did this so well, and this, and this. You might want to adjust that. But your speech was so good because of this!"

Praise is much more effective than criticism.

In short, there is a time for criticism, there really is, but make sure it's the right time before you jump to the conclusion that addressing that flaw in the other person is the only way. Sometimes, the best thing is to fully ignore that thing, and to focus on complimenting the good things instead.

If you're working with a person who can't seem to get a task right, no matter how hard he tries, and even praise doesn't help the situation, sometimes the best option before criticizing is simply to give him a new task or focus.

It may be easier to send one of these messages, but it is far harder to receive.

Maybe he doesn't really need to be good at that specific task, or maybe you're just not the one who needs to teach him. As we have said, criticism is a very powerful tool, very effective when the time is right, but it can also be very damaging. Criticism is something, unlike praise, that you should be very wary of using.

Don't jump into criticism. If criticism seems necessary in a certain situation, give it some real thought (and follow the guideline of making sure there isn't a better way) before using it.

Two: Put time on your side. There is usually a right time and a right place for criticism. As mentioned, criticism is best done one-on-one. If you can help it, don't announce your concerns in front of the kids or workers. Take the child or person to a private place and talk to him individually.

Another part of putting time on your side is to only criticize in a face-to-face setting. This is crucial: If at all possible, find a time when you can meet in person. Messages, e-mails, voice mails, and texts are off limits for criticism. To repeat: these are *off limits!*

> **Criticism should always take place in a setting where response and interaction are welcome and possible.**

Really, it may be easier for you to say what you need to say through an electronic message, but it is more likely to cause hurt, misunderstandings, resentment, and other negatives. And as we have said about all communication, it is a two-way connection. It may be easier to send one of these messages, but it is far harder to receive. Criticism should always take place in a setting where response and interaction are welcome and possible.

Putting time on your side also means dealing with the issue quickly, in a timely fashion. You don't want to criticize someone for a mistake he made months ago. On the other hand, if waiting another day means you'll be able to meet with him in person, waiting can help. But don't wait too long. Just as with apologies, criticism needs to be done sooner rather than later.

Three: The last thing to really focus on is the effectiveness of criticism. Don't just say what you think you should say. Tell the other person what they need to hear in order to change and improve. This is like apologizing in that it's not only about what you say; it's more about what they *hear* and *feel*. So think it through, and really focus on saying the right thing in the right way. You want to help the person, not cause hurt or worsen your relationship with him.

If criticism really is the best choice, be sure you do it humbly, carefully, and caringly. Making the other person feel respected, valued, and loved is vital to successful and truly constructive criticism. Before you communicate, think about what he really needs and what will really help!

PART SIX

MEDIUMS OF COMMUNICATION

"Texting is a fundamentally sneaky form of communication...."
—Lynne Truss

KNOW YOUR COMMUNICATION MEDIUMS

*"What you do daily is part of what
you become permanently."*
—CHRIS BRADY

From Small Talk to Strategy

There are many different ways to communicate, just as there are many different mediums of communication. While many of them are discussed in this book, there are a few guidelines that must be understood about all mediums of communication, even as we learn which mediums to use in the right situations and how to apply each medium most effectively.

For example, on the topic of small talk, which can be an important part of effective communication in many settings (from romance and home to work and business), communication coach Leil Lowndes taught the following:

> Small talk is music, not facts.
> It is melody, not words.
> Relax, and match the mood.

Another way to say this is that to be effective at small talk, focus on how things *feel*—not on the specific words, details, or plans that are outlined. To accomplish this, try the following key to great small talk: Ask the other person about what he likes. Really listen, really care, and really pay attention.

Most people like talking about themselves and their interests, and this is a relaxed way to get to know each other.

Important Guidelines

More generally, in all mediums of communication, learn and apply the following guidelines:

A) *Don't rely too much on any one medium.*

This is important. Imagine a person who only sends Facebook messages when trying to get ahold of people. Or someone who only uses e-mail or even live chat.

Indeed, imagine someone who only communicates through public speaking. To express a concern to his wife, he might have to get up on the checkout stand at the grocery store and announce to everyone how he is feeling!

If you rely entirely on one method of communication, you'll consistently decrease your own effectiveness.

Though not all mediums of communication seem this extreme, all of them *can* be this awkward if *taken* to extremes. As Chris Brady put it, you might be stretching yourself a bit thin if you express love to your wife in an e-mail…unless this is just one of the many ways you tell her you love her.

Another example: You might not want to accuse someone of something big on Twitter. And the list only continues. There are certain mediums of communication that are simply better used for certain things than others.

If you rely entirely (or almost entirely) on one method of communication, you'll consistently decrease your own effectiveness.

B) Know what medium the other person prefers, and try to accommodate him.

You'll hear this one repeated a few times, because it is actually a very important part of picking the best communication mediums. Yes, there are certain methods you prefer, but as a leader one of your main purposes is to help ensure that all communication is as effective as possible. Figure out which medium(s) the other person prefers, and try using it (or them) whenever possible.

C) Use the medium that will be most effective given the current type of communication and the specific circumstances.

Know when to use social media. When to send a letter. When to call on the phone. And when to send an e-mail. As you read through the rest of Part Six, we hope it will help in defining what uses each medium best serves. But a lot of it is simply common sense.

Communication Levels

In addition, and this is very important, keep in mind that since communication is all about connection, and connection is a matter of energy, the highest levels of communication are naturally the most energetic. Use this to your advantage.

For example, author Michael J. Lerner taught that different kinds of communication can be ranked according to their ability to impact people:

Low Levels of Impact
Advertising, Impersonal Direct Mail, Indirect Electronic Communication (television, radio, online ads, etc.)

Medium Levels of Impact
Direct Electronic Communication (voice messages, e-mails, texts, etc.), Handwritten Notes

High Levels of Impact
Phone Calls, Face-to-Face Conversations, In-Person Chats Online, Events and Seminars

Note that "higher impact" communications aren't necessarily *better*. They are certainly better if what you need is high impact, but sometimes you just want to pass on a quick bit of information, and in such cases "low impact" communication is more effective for everyone. Indeed, when you have a minor point to share and you turn it into a major production to obtain high impact, it just creates a lot of drama.

Nonverbal Messages

Another "high level" of impact comes in nonverbal communication. This applies in nearly all the mediums of communication, especially those where you are visible or audible as you communicate. Joseph A. DeVito taught in *The Interpersonal Communication Book* that some of the most important aspects of any communication include:

- Verbal Elements [things you actually say]
- Emotional Elements [the energy you exude as you say it]
- Nonverbal Elements [the things the other person hears, sees, or feels, regardless of what you actually say]

Of the three, the emotional elements of communication are usually more powerful and memorable than what you actually say, and the nonverbal messages you share (on purpose or unwittingly) are the most powerful and memorable of all.

Some communication coaches suggest ways to improve unspoken elements of your communication skills. But piece-by-piece attempts to, for example, make better gestures as you speak or stand taller when you're listening to someone seldom last.

Instead, the best communicators effectively use nonverbal elements naturally, without

Get your message right. Know what you stand for, what your real message is. This is essential in all communication, if you want it to be effective.

giving them conscious emphasis during each conversation. The way to improve this natural trait is to focus on being congruent.

Congruence

There are at least three steps to this:

The first key to congruency is to get your message right. Know what you stand for, what your real message is. This is essential in all communication, if you want it to be effective.

Second, use symbols, stories, examples, ideas, words, and behaviors that are congruent with your real message. Walk the talk. Be the message. Live it.

Third, with the first two keys above firmly in place, practice. Practice a lot. Whatever mediums of communication you use today and this week and this month, remember to get your message right and to use the kind of examples, symbols, and everyday morals that are in keeping with your message. Do this over and over. Applying the communication rules outlined in this book will help you accomplish this.

The natural result of such congruence is that your nonverbal cues will fall increasingly into place—often very quickly. If you aren't congruent in your message, your words, and the way you live your life, it's difficult if not impossible to get your nonverbal communications in line.

On the other hand, congruence will improve your nonverbal communication. Note that congruence will also greatly increase your credibility in many situations.

Finally, once you are living and applying all three of these keys, and your congruence is increasing, it might be helpful to get feedback from a mentor, spouse, close friend, or other trusted advisor on ways to improve your nonverbal communication. But be sure to get the three keys outlined above working *before* turning your attention to techniques.

Conclusion

With this basic overview of communication mediums in mind, it's time to discuss some of the most important mediums and how we can improve the way we utilize each. Since we discussed face-to-face conversations at length in the first five parts of this book, we won't repeat it here. But the remaining mediums of communication are very important.

> **Whatever mediums of communication you use today and this week and this month, remember to get your message right.**

RULE #25

MASTER PUBLIC SPEAKING

*"I am convinced that public speaking is
something anyone can master."*

—CHRIS BRADY

Stand Up and Wow Them!

To this point in the book we've jokingly focused a lot on your "acting career" and the idea that it is where you've been most successful in your life, but we should probably mention that you also happen to be a very effective public speaker as well. Oh yes, you're fantastic! You wow the crowd every time with your finesse and power with words and emotion.

You may be thinking, "Public speaking? Now why on earth would I do *that*?" But what you might not realize is that throughout your life, you've had many opportunities to speak in public, and you've become quite exceptional. Or if not, you can start now.

But it's not just you. Sadly, a lot of people are afraid to speak, even to their family. It's not that they don't want to be good public speakers; it's just that they're afraid of it. An old saying assures us that most people are more afraid of public speaking than death. As Jerry Seinfeld put it, "If you have to go to a funeral, you're better off in the casket than giving the eulogy!"

How sad is this? With all these opportunities to speak and inspire others, most people would do anything to avoid speaking in public.

In a book on communication, public speaking is a vital topic. To be sure, public speaking requires communication, the two-way connection between humans, but improving this skill is immeasurably worth it.

Invest in Speaking

If you learn more about the art and science of public speaking and actually work on improving your abilities, the normal outcome is more trust and more authority from others, better promotions, bigger projects to manage, increased creation, more joy, and less stress.

Moreover, working on this skill will help you see things coming that would have blindsided you before. You'll be amazed by how your life can be positively impacted by better public speaking and more effective communication. The study of communication and public speaking will expand your life. The way you communicate and your leadership ability can get you everywhere.

> **With all these opportunities to speak and inspire others, most people would do anything to avoid speaking in public.**

The fact is, those who are better public speakers tend to be more effective communicators in general. If you can connect to each member in an audience as you speak, how much easier is it to connect to one person?

Get to the Heart

It is important to speak to the heart of your audience and to your message. And a great key to this is to stay on task. You're speaking for a reason. Focus on that. As Chris Brady said, "Just because something happened doesn't make it funny or pertinent." What we share really needs to be relevant and have a point to it. If we spend ten minutes telling a side story and then finally get back to the main point, the distraction usually takes away from the impact of the main message.

> **Those who are better public speakers tend to be more effective communicators in general.**

On the other hand, one of the best ways to speak to people's hearts and have a lasting impact is through the stories you tell. People connect with stories that have relevance to situations in their lives or to the message you're sharing.

So share stories, but only those that have to do with your message or the situation of the people you're speaking to—because let's be clear, if your message is directed at them, then connecting with them is part of your message.

You also need to truly care about the people you're speaking to. They'll feel either your genuine concern for them or the lack of it.

Getting to the heart means focusing on the other people and doing or saying whatever you can to help them.

Above all, it is essential to transfer the right *feeling* when you speak. Effective public speakers leave their listeners with a sense of something powerful, a feeling that lasts.

> **Getting to the heart means focusing on the other people and doing or saying whatever you can to help them.**

Indeed, top leaders learn to help those they speak to catch a vision or feeling of what's possible for them. Such speakers convey the truth with their own passion and energy so it lasts.

Conclusion

There are, of course, other guidelines that will help you increase your public speaking ability. This is a very important facet of good communication. In fact, if you want to really *master* public speaking—and top leaders need this skill—we'll give you a powerful suggestion below on where to learn more.

But first, let's focus again on the main point of public speaking. Why does it matter? How does it help communication? Why should anyone who isn't planning on being a professional orator work to get good at it?

The answer is that communication is about leadership, and public speaking is a great way to improve both.

As we stretch ourselves into new and sometimes even uncomfortable situations such as learning to be a better public speaker, we will grow and become better prepared to have an impact on the world in whatever field we pursue. Learning to speak in public nearly always helps you better communicate one on one, and the very same skills often apply.

So take a deep breath. It's fun. It's wonderful. It's hard at times. But we like to think that giving a eulogy shouldn't be a person's worst nightmare.

More important: Effective public speaking will almost definitely improve the power of your communication, your leadership, and your success in life.

***

NOTE: Effective public speaking improves the power of your communication and increases your leadership skills, victories, and achievements. LIFE Leadership Essential Series offers an excellent book that provides a full training workshop on public speaking. It is enjoyable, easy to understand and apply, and very effective. If you want or need to upgrade your public speaking, don't miss it! The book is entitled:

SPLASH: A Leader's Guide to Effective Public Speaking.

It is available at www.lifeleadership.com.

RULE #26

PUT THE "LIVE" INTO LIVE CHAT

"The Internet is the most important single development
in the history of human communication
since the invention of call waiting."
—DAVE BARRY

What It Is

There are many technologies in our modern world that allow for long distance communication. Live chat (or video calls) includes those where you can see and hear the other person in a live setting through electronic means, and at least some of the participants can interact with each other in real time.

Because you can both see and hear the other person, in some ways live chat is the closest thing to real face-to-face communication. As a result, most of the same rules apply. But there are some differences, and extra guidelines that should also be addressed. These include:

A) If you have something really difficult, or momentous—such as an award to present, or criticism to give—it's usually best to meet with the other person directly, not just face-to-face in live chat, but also in person.

When you're actually there with the person, the emotions, feelings and your ability to read him is different, and though many times live chat is acceptable, there are certainly times when direct in-person communication is far superior.

If it is simply a matter of informing the other person that you have something to present him, or you need to cover some quick information, live chat is probably fine. But if your conversation promises to be difficult or amazing, doing it in person will show how much you care. And it will be much more effective.

B) Live Chat can be a good medium for a speech or an interview where only a few people do the talking, but if there's to be a social gathering, a committee meeting, or a group of people who all need to talk, live chat is probably not as good as an in-person meeting.

In choosing between live chat and in-person meetings, weigh the balance between personal connection and the need to hold the conversation frequently from long distances.

C) Control your technology. Though Live Chat is a good venue for long distance communication, if the Internet connection is failing or if the video isn't working correctly, , then perhaps a phone call would work best.

D) Pay attention to your background. This is simple, but it can make a big difference. If you're to be interviewed for an important job, and all the other person can see in the background behind you is a bunch of *Transformers* posters, well, maybe that's not the best thing to communicate. Or maybe it is, if you're interviewing for a job selling toys. Pay attention to the details.

SIDEBAR TO READER:

We're not judging you for those posters. Chris Brady himself admits to having posters of the band Kiss on his wall (many years ago, not now), and many people have never taken down those My Little Pony or Backstreet Boys posters.

Of course, if you have teenage daughters, you might instead have One Direction posters in your home. We're not judging. We're just suggesting that you not go into your daughter's room and sit on her bed with the boy band posters behind you while you interview someone in online chat for an important job.

Of course, controlling your background doesn't only mean the posters or the color of paint on your wall. It can be as simple as the environment of the room around you. If your kids are screaming—or even singing One Direction songs—and your husband is doing yoga in the background, or if the phone keeps ringing, you can see how this could hurt or even compromise your communication. So control the environment, not just the background.

E) Dress appropriately. Yes, this same rule applies. If they can see you, then you need to be dressed for the occasion—whatever occasion it may be.

For phone communication, perhaps dress isn't as important, although many top leaders have found that dressing for the occasion helps them do well, no matter who else is around to see it. If it helps your confidence and if it fits the occasion, then you're probably good to dress up a bit. As always, be professional.

F) If important decisions are made on the live chat, whether in a speech with hundreds of people or in a meeting with only a few, it is important to have a scribe or someone else to take notes on the important information and then to distribute it to the appropriate people by e-mail or text.

G) Along with this, if the meeting is with a group, it's good to text or e-mail a reminder about the date and time of the meeting beforehand. People tend to forget video calls even more easily than they forget in-person meetings.

Again, it's important to remember that most of the other rules of direct in-person communication will also apply to live chats, so read the chapters pertaining to the other modes of communication, and see how and where they apply in this medium.

RULE #27

UPGRADE YOUR PHONE COMMUNICATION

"As we grow up in more technology-enriched environments filled with laptops and smartphones, technology is not just becoming a part of our daily lives—it's becoming a part of each and every one of us."
—ADORA SVITAK

Time to Talk

We live in a day and age when you can talk to someone hundreds or even thousands of miles away, literally hear them, and communicate with them—and all directly, in real time. This is an amazing development, and of course using the phone to communicate can be a very good thing. But as with all forms of communication, some guidelines should be followed in order to ensure the most effective communication.

In this chapter, we'll cover some of the most basic and important guidelines for quality phone communication and discuss how best to communicate with people over the phone.

A) Start with the obvious.

It's nice to be thoughtful and polite. It's very easy when calling someone to simply think about the reason you're calling and what you have to say to her. But this can be a mistake if you ignore something obvious in your life, or that of the person you're calling, and simply jump into your point. For example, if you haven't spoken to the person in a long time, but when she says hello, you immediately launch into your business reason for calling, it can come across as selfish and out of touch.

If a wedding has recently taken place in the person's family, perhaps ask how things are going for the new couple. If a funeral has happened, ask how the family is doing.

Chris Brady suggests that if you call someone you haven't talked to in a while, maybe start out with "Hey, I'm calling for a reason, but first, it's been forever! How are you doing? What's going on in your life these days?" and really take a moment to catch up before getting to your "reason."

This is helpful because it makes it clear to the person that you do have a point and you want to get to it at some time during the conversation, but it also gives him an opportunity to feel a connection with you, and it lets him know you really care about him and not just whatever it is you're calling about.

Of course, this doesn't have to happen with every phone call. If you're calling someone back ten minutes after the last call, or if it's only been a few hours or even days since you've seen (or talked to) the person, you might not need to worry so much about catching up.

SIDEBAR TO READER:

"Hey, I'm calling for a reason, but first, it's been forever! How are you? What's new and different in your life?"

"Um…it's been two minutes…not much has changed…"

Strange. Just sayin'….

B) Don't waste their time.

This one goes right along with the first guideline above, and it can be difficult to find the right balance, but it's important that we do so.

Seriously, don't waste their time. You are calling for a reason. Don't spend twenty minutes catching up unless it really serves both of you to do so. If it's just you not getting to the point, you should fix that.

Learn how to convey words with brevity. Over time learn how to say what you want to say and do it with the fewest words possible.

"Starting with the obvious" is taking a second to focus on the other person and give him your attention. But "not wasting their time" also means getting to the point. Again, find a balance between these two guidelines.

C) Handle it in the most effective way.

We've mentioned this in earlier chapters, but as we're focusing directly on phone communication, it's worth remembering.

Be sure you're using the most effective medium of communication to get your message across. If it's something that should really be handled face to face, then you shouldn't do it on a phone call.

This applies to the opposite extreme as well. If your point would be better communicated through a text message, then send a text message. Phone calls can be intrusive. They break into whatever the other person may be doing at the time, causing him to focus on you instead. If what you have to say could be handled more effectively through an e-mail or text, then again, we suggest you don't waste his time by calling.

As you're picking mediums, however, you should really have some idea of what works best for the other person and what mediums of communication she actually prefers.

Chris Brady shares an example of how he's had people become angry at him for not responding to their Facebook messages, but as Brady puts it, he doesn't spend time looking through the hundreds of Facebook messages he receives. Facebook messaging is simply not his medium of communication.

Since good communication means more than merely saying something, because it requires that the other person *receive* it, be wise: pick mediums that you've learned will work best for the other person.

For example, ask them if they receive text messages before sending one. Don't wait on an answer to an e-mail until you discover (months later) that they never check their e-mail. In short, where possible, know the person you're communicating with and which mediums will work best for her.

> **To improve your phone communication, simply remember to act like the owner when you're on a phone call.**

D) Take notes.

If you're on a phone call with important details that you'll want to remember, such as legal matters, or if you discuss anything technical, it can be good to take notes on what is said. Often it's helpful to write down the time, date, and name of the person you are talking to, and other important details that take place in the conversation.

This is a simple rule, but it can really help when it's needed.

E) Act like the owner.

Though an employee may feel little need to please the customer, business owners frequently go far out of their way to please every client. To improve your phone communication, simply remember to act like the owner when you're on a phone call.

Go out of your way to make it comfortable for the other person or people. If they're having trouble hearing you, find a way to make it work. Be the one to take charge, no matter the challenge, and really act like the owner. Help and serve, and work to make the phone call effective.

F) Share the context.

If you're in the airport and the intercom keeps going off, or if you're in a crowd of people and can't hear very well, or if you're driving and you have the phone on speaker with other people around, let the person on the other end of the line know.

"I'm in an airport and it's noisy. Sorry. Do you want to continue or should I call you back when I'm in a quieter place?"

Share the context of the situation you're in. Explain why he'll keep hearing announcements or why you keep asking him "What?" And especially if you're on a speaker, let the other person know who else might hear him when he speaks.

This is part of being the owner, and making it comfortable for the other person. Share the context of your situation so the person you're communicating with isn't confused about what's going on.

SIDEBAR TO READER:

Interesting fact: While the main topics spouses argue about are still money, intimacy, and children, researchers have discovered that "smartphone use is rapidly rising on the list." In one study, a majority of participants "reported that phones, computers, and other devices were significantly disrupting their relationships and family lives."

Part of good communication, especially for leaders, is not ignoring the person (or people) you are with right now by constantly looking at your phone, sending texts during an important conversation, or otherwise putting electronic interaction ahead of the people sitting or standing right in front of you.

If you need to, excuse yourself to take an important call or text, and then return to the conversation ready to focus. Doing so is much better than disrespecting those you are trying to communicate with.

G) Control your technology.

Again, you're the owner. Don't pick a plan with limited minutes and then silently criticize the service provider for ending an important phone call. Don't forget to empty your voice mail box and then get angry when you didn't get an important message.

If your ringtone is set to the song *I'm Too Sexy* and you're going into an important business meeting where you might not want that being heard, change your ringtone or turn off the ringer.

You're the owner, you're the one in control, and you're the one responsible for your technology.

H) Apply all other rules of communication that are applicable.

We've already shared a number of important rules and principles of communication in this book, and as you use different mediums for communication, make sure you apply all of them that are applicable to each medium. Use common sense, and think about communication and what works best.

As we said before, this is the world we live in, and it's a world with a lot of technologies. There are many forms and mediums for communication, and it can be hard to master all of them. But to really understand any form of communication, we need to follow the principles and apply the rules, and anyone who does so will likely be amazed by the positive results.

RULE #28

FIND THE RIGHT BALANCE IN CHAT ROOMS AND SOCIAL MEDIA

*"Social media is changing the way we communicate
and the way we are perceived, both positively and negatively.
Every time you post a photo, or update your status,
you are contributing to your own digital footprint
and personal brand."*

—AMY JO MARTIN

THE NEW RULES

Social media is an epidemic, for good and ill. It has taken over the world. A person without a Facebook account or a business without a Web page is rare in many circles. And as the world has turned to the Internet, an increasing number of people have turned to social media.

Let's be clear, as we said previously: This is the world we live in, so use it. Use social media to grow your business and increase your range of community. Use it to socialize and have fun with friends. If you want to, use it to update people on the status of your life—whether you're getting married or had a taco this morning. Whatever works for your relationships, business, and life.

Social media has become a big influence in the world, and it can be a good thing for you, if you decide to use it. But be wise about it. For example: you probably shouldn't rely on it for all your communication, and there are definitely some guidelines that should be followed when you do utilize social media. These rules really matter. For example:

A) Don't let your actions on social media ruin your reputation.

As we said, social media can be very helpful in upping your reputation or growing your business/career, but a lot of people do this wrong. In fact, many end up doing quite the opposite.

There are several facets of this. The quotes you share, the tweets/status updates, the pictures, and even anything you like or just pass on—it all reflects on your reputation. People see it and draw conclusions from it.

For example, you really don't want to share your swim-suit selfies on social media or anything like this. Really, just don't. Your business partners or potential employers will be able to see them, and it could really affect your professional life. Don't wade into this kind of silliness.

B) Don't say dumb things.

> **The quotes you share, the tweets/status updates, the pictures, and even anything you like or just pass on—it all reflects on your reputation.**

This should be applied to any forms or mediums of communication, but especially on social media, the dumb things you say can reflect very badly upon you—and many people are able to see them.

How often do you see on the news that some government or corporate official gets into a lot of trouble for saying dumb things, even in simple e-mails, but also with tweets or other posts? A lot of people have access to this social platform that represents you. Again: many people have the ability to see the dumb things that are posted. Top leaders just avoid saying offensive or inappropriate things in the first place.

C) Be wise about privacy.

This is very important and should go without saying, but we'll mention it anyway. If you need to give out your address, bank account number, or other sensitive information that could be used against you, don't do it on social media, where everyone can see it. Simply find a better medium. Or better still, don't give it out electronically at all. At the very least, be sure that if you do share sensitive information, it is on a secure site.

Also, be careful about posting your travel plans or allowing sites to inform the whole world of your exact whereabouts.

You should probably teach your children and youth to be very careful about these things as well.

D) Remember that electronic communications are public.

If something needs to be communicated in private, do it face to face. Nothing communicated online may ultimately be private. Even something as simple as a voice message left on an electronic messaging device can sometimes be accessed by third parties.

> **If something needs to be communicated in private, do it face to face.**

For example, in *The Atlantic,* Walter Kirn tells the story of how he left a message on his wife's phone asking her where to find walnuts in the kitchen during breakfast, only to have his phone quickly post an ad about walnuts.[13] This happens a lot in the new "data mining" era.[14] Advertisers are increasingly responsive to keywords in e-mails, texts, posts, etc., which trigger an ad or recommendation for their goods and services.[15]

What you say and do online is available to third parties. Asked whether a hack of all e-mails in their company could happen, 74 percent of a panel of experts and executives in Silicon Valley Tech companies said yes.[16] Even leading governments sometimes get hacked. So if you need to discuss something that should be secret, be careful about using electronic communication.

Again, we should make the point clear that social media can be very useful and that you really should use it in many situations to promote your business or to help build relationships. Social media is obviously not the best way to build strong, close relationships. But it can be very helpful if what's needed in a certain business relationship is to take it to a more social level when you're not quite clicking well with someone.

Chat Rooms

Note that we're including both chat rooms and social media in this chapter together, because many of the same rules apply, and at the very least, they're very similar. We've already covered many of the main guidelines of social media communication, so now let's move to chat rooms.

To be quite honest, there are few circumstances where chat rooms are the best format for communication. On the one hand, it's live. On the other hand, you can't see or hear the people in them. Therefore, it is both live and a bit impersonal.

This format or medium of communication is the weakest of the personal and the weakest of the *impersonal*. Unlike e-mailing, communication through a chat room doesn't allow the other person the opportunity to ignore the message and wait to respond until later—which makes it weak for the impersonal.

That said, there *are* times to use it. Perhaps someone you're working with really prefers it. Oftentimes using a chat room can be helpful when you and the other person are working on a project together that's in written form or on art or diagrams that you both want to look at during the conversation—or when you want to learn from a crowd of strangers which model year used Hummer to buy, for instance.

Another time chat rooms might be helpful is if technological or geographical differences simply make it more accessible (e.g., you don't have access to other options).

In general, if it's a quick thing, go ahead and use a chat room. Otherwise, you can use it to move to another medium. "Hey, I've got something to send to you. What's your e-mail address?" Or "Hey, let's jump to a video call!"

This can be very helpful. Because the chat room is live, the other person is able to respond right away and then follow up on e-mail—or you can both move to another more personal medium of communication.

RULE #29

MAGNIFY MESSAGES WITH AUDIO, TEXT, AND E-MAIL

"Texting has added a new dimension to language use, but its long-term impact is negligible. It is not a disaster."
—DAVID CRYSTAL

THE NEW MEDIA

Messages in any form, including voice, text, or even e-mails, require serious care. A lot of miscommunication can take place in messages because they're not live, the other person doesn't always have the ability to respond in the moment, and you don't have the opportunity to clarify yourself if she does misunderstand.

Obviously texts, e-mails, and audio messages are useful mediums of communication that should be taken advantage of under the right circumstances, but certain guidelines should be followed to ensure that no feelings are hurt or relationships ruined and that the best communication can take place. These include:

A) Never leave a negative message or comment.

We can't stress the "never" enough. Without interaction and feedback, and without the ability to hear your tone of voice or to respond, any negatives communicated in these formats are drastically amplified. This is true even though the person leaving the message may not realize it is happening.

These messages frequently sound or read as much more terse and angry than the person who left them intended, and this can cause a lot of unnecessarily negative feelings.

The strongest message you should ever leave in these formats is "I really need to talk to you. Please call ASAP."

For example, add even one more *really* to this, and you've made it too strong: "I really, really need to talk to you. Please call ASAP."

The amplifiers make it seem bigger than it is, which leaves the other person's mind to brainstorm every possible negative. If it's a minor issue, that's a very inconsiderate thing to do to them. If it's a major one, you probably just made it a lot worse.

The example above is ineffective communication and also ineffective leadership. Worse, if you do this routinely, it can turn into downright bad leadership.

SIDEBAR TO READER:

Earlier we mentioned the boy who cried wolf. Well, imagine if that boy was the leader of the Sheep Herding Company and frequently sent out urgent messages to his employees or business partners.

"HURRY! THIS IS IMPORTANT! I NEED YOU TO GET OVER HERE RIGHT NOW OR THIS WOLF WILL EAT ALL OF OUR SHEEP!!!"

After even one such false message, any repeats are likely to be pointedly disregarded.

B) E-mail is a good medium for long, detailed messages, with lots of material or deep stuff, or if it needs to be edited or considered. (Note that this does not apply to audio messages. If you try to leave important details in audio messages, you'll find that many of them are lost or forgotten. As mentioned, the most detail you really want to leave in an audio message is a callback number.)

C) Texting is helpful for ongoing yet unobtrusive communication. It has the ability to occur in a live back-and-forth, but it also allows the other person to answer whenever it is most convenient.

D) Audio messages usually aren't that useful when trying to communicate any more than "Hey, give me a call back, please." Of course, if it's just a reminder of an appointment or a quick answer to a question, there's definitely a time when it can be the best medium. For example, you *can* hear the speaker's tone of voice in an audio message, and sometimes the other person needs to hear your enthusiasm or excitement, even if all you're saying is "Give me a call when you get a chance."

E) As always, it's helpful to know what medium of communication the other person prefers (texts, e-mails, whatever), and to use it when possible.

F) Lastly, please read all other guidelines from the previous chapter, "Find the Right Balance in Chat Rooms and Social Media." They all apply to texts, e-mails, and audio messages as well.

RULE #30

BRING BACK CLASSY LETTERS AND GREETING CARDS

*"A friendship can weather most things and thrive in thin soil;
but it needs a little mulch of letters and phone calls and small,
silly presents every so often—just to save it
from drying out completely."*
—PAM BROWN

THE POWER OF THE PEN

Writing letters…a lost art. There was a time, long ago, when letters were really the only form of long distance communication, and they were often used to communicate to those in close proximity as well.

People once used letters to express love, gratitude, fear, angst. They used letters to tell stories and ask questions. Letters were used for business, social, and personal purposes. They were used among friends, family, and co-workers.

In the world today, the writing of letters truly has become a lost art, because there are so many more "efficient" or "effective" mediums of communication. But there is still certainly a time for letters.

Hopefully we all still have that grandparent or friend who sends greeting cards every year on our birthday. She always includes some heartfelt line shared in her own handwriting in the card. And we've all gotten these cards and wondered why she didn't just call or post "Happy

Birthday!" on our wall on Facebook. But there's something personal and precious about handwritten letters or greeting cards. There's something truly special about them.

Indeed, there is a reason they were used as communication for so long, and have somehow managed to last even now—although it's clear their use has diminished. And this reason isn't just that mobile phones hadn't been invented.

In this chapter, we want to do something a little different. Rather than go through the guidelines of writing and using letters and greeting cards, we want to spend more time on why they matter and what makes them so great and important.

Allow us to share several letters from novels and history, from lovers and friends, and let's just look at why this lost art should be brought back, at least to some degree, and how you might want to use it to improve your communication.

Take a look at this excerpt of a letter from Abigail to John Adams:

> *My Dearest Friend,*
>
> *...should I draw you the picture of my Heart, it would be what I hope you still would Love; tho it contained nothing new; the early possession you obtained there; and the absolute power you have ever maintained over it; leaves not the smallest space unoccupied. I look back to the early days of our acquaintance; and Friendship, as to the days of Love and Innocence; and with an indescribable pleasure*

I have seen near a score of years roll over our Heads, with an affection heightened and improved by time — nor have the dreary years of absence in the smallest degree effaced from my mind the Image of the dear untitled man to whom I gave my Heart...

If you know much about the relationship between John and Abigail Adams, you know they sent over a thousand letters to one another over the course of the years while John was away founding a country. They managed to retain a long distance relationship — on and off — throughout the years, largely by sending each other letters.

> **It is amazing how much a person can express in writing, how much a letter can convey and make others feel.**

Funny, considering that nowadays — with all the many mediums for instant long distance communication — so many relationships are lost because not enough communication takes place. Even with video calls, live chat, smartphones, social media and plenty of texting, people struggle to make relationships survive long distance for very long.

Yet in history, just as with John and Abigail, many people strengthened their love and commitment for one another over many years, often sustaining or reviving the bond by a few letters here and there.

It's Special

It is amazing how much a person can express in writing, how much a letter can convey and make others feel. We've made it clear in other chapters that it's good to use different mediums of communication for different purposes, and because sending letters is slow and unreliable, it isn't the best medium for most business communication.

But in keeping relationships alive, including some key business relationships, it can make all the difference. Sending your business partners a birthday or thank you card every year usually really does mean just a bit more than posting "happy birthday" on their wall.

It's special. Letters and greeting cards can be personal in ways no audio or voice message can really convey, and you certainly can't say the same things on social media that you can in a letter to someone you love.

Here's another excerpt of a letter from Abigail to John that we found rather interesting:

> I have sometimes been ready to think that the passion for Liberty cannot be Equally Strong in the Breasts of those who have been accustomed to deprive their fellow Creatures of theirs. Of this I am certain that it is not founded upon that generous and Christian principal of doing to others as we would that others should do unto us.

Amazing, isn't it, how she's able to express some of her deepest beliefs to her husband in a simple letter? And in so few words. She's able to bare her heart and make a profound statement of belief.

For some reason, it can be easier at times to write down your beliefs in letters than to say them straight out, or to post them on social media. But here it is done beautifully, and this is just one example of many.

More Examples

Let's take a look at another letter, from *Pride and Prejudice*, written by Mr. Darcy to Elizabeth Bennett:

> *Be not alarmed, madam, on receiving this letter, by the apprehension of its containing any repetition of those sentiments or renewal of those offers which were last night so disgusting to you. I write without any intention of paining you, or humbling myself, by dwelling on wishes which, for the happiness of both, cannot be too soon forgotten: and the effort which the formation and the perusal of this letter must occasion, should have been spared had not my character required it to be written and read. You must, therefore, pardon the freedom with which I demand your attention; your feelings, I know, will bestow it unwillingly, but I demand it of your justice.*

Wow, that's good. Obviously a lot of its delicacy has to do with the refinement of the language, but even using smaller words, writing out this sort of statement in a letter can be so much more romantic and effective than, say, sending a text message.

SIDEBAR TO READER:

Seriously, imagine if Mr. Darcy had sent this text to Elizabeth:

"Don't freak out about this text. I don't want to remind you of how lame and offensive I was last night when we talked. I absolutely don't want to bother you more than I already have. But I wasn't wrong about everything, and I really needed to write this text to make sure you understand. I really hope you will read it. So yeah, sorry, because I was wrong about some things, for sure. But not others."

Very romantic, isn't it?

Not!

As we've said, the writing of letters is a beautiful art, and it can still, even today, be an effective way to communicate and build relationships with those you care about. Obviously, as with all the other mediums of communication, it shouldn't be the *only* medium you use. In fact, a rare letter is special largely because it's so rare! Don't worry about flowery language; just handwrite a short note. It will be special. It's good to send greeting cards and write letters. You should do it. So go ahead and do it.

Indeed, if you ever need to really connect with someone (to apologize, express great love or admiration, etc.), consider writing a heartfelt letter.

We could share many other examples of letters long ago written, but let's try and apply more of the language that would be used today. Of course the language and tone of past letters was often very beautiful, but that wasn't all that made letter writing so wonderful. Even today we can write letters and get through to the hearts of people, using words we all actually understand.

Take a look at this letter from a woman to her unborn child:

> *My dearest son, I don't know your name yet, or exactly what you look like, but I can already tell your heart. I already know you're amazing. I already know you're beautiful. In a few weeks, I'll finally see your face, and you'll get to know the faces of your father and I as well. We can't yet promise, my son, to be the perfect parents, but we do promise that we will try. We will love you with everything in us, and will work to give you the best life possible. Were we in control of it, I think your father and I would wish no pain, hardships or struggles into your life.*
>
> *Then again, we have come to know over the years that pain and hardship brings about change, and truly, change is necessary for growth. Still, I wish I could protect you always, have you close to me as I do now, protected, safe and warm. But I know you will be born to influence more than just mine and your father's lives, so someday we'll have to let you go. But know that we are always here, my son, and that no matter what happens, we will always love you.*

To be quite honest, this baby won't even fully understand this letter until years later, when he himself has become a man and gone off into the world. Perhaps a letter that isn't received until decades later could be called "inefficient." Talk about snail mail! But just think, when this letter is received, it will likely mean far more in the life of this man than a text that says, "You're cool, son. I like you."

There is certainly a time for letters in relationships. What about this greeting card from a man to his best friend,

> *Joe, we've known each other a long time. We've shared a lot of birthdays. We've shared a lot of great memories. I'm sad to say I can't be there for this one. Work, the kids, my busy life. I hate to say that it sometimes takes precedence over you, but you're the man of the family yourself, so you understand. Just wanted to let you know I'm thinking of you, even though I can't be around for your party. Make sure to be extra dumb for me, man. Stuff your face with cake and enjoy the game. Make sure you let your Mrs. know you love her, because what are birthdays really about?*

The expression of friendship and admiration just wouldn't mean the same in an e-mail or a text or even an audio message. A letter or card will likely be kept and reread. On this day when a friend couldn't be there, this letter probably meant more to Joe than a virtual e-mail birthday cake ever could.

In fact, it doesn't have to be that personal to make a difference. Check out this thank you card between practical strangers:

Dear whoever you are. I see you every morning at your desk, and I feel bad I've never actually said hi. But I wanted to thank you for the smile you gave me earlier as I passed you. I was on the phone, and having a pretty hard day, but your smile made a difference. Thanks again.

A thank you card for a smile? Whose day was made now? Whoever that person at the front desk is, this card left quietly on his desk while he went to lunch will certainly bring a smile back to his face when he returns. A simple greeting card could be the start of a friendship. And at the very least, it could make a person's day.

> **Letters and greeting cards are hardly used anymore, but we suggest that if you want to form long, deep, and lasting relationships, you find a place for them in your communication.**

Even with the very impersonal beginning, starting with "whoever you are," this simple letter will likely have much more of an impact than, say, if this man were to smile back the next time he passed this person's desk. Both are good, but the card is special.

Letters and greeting cards are hardly used anymore, but we suggest that if you want to form long, deep, and lasting relationships, you find a place for them in your communication. Most of us use texting, calling, chatting, and social media. Far fewer people find a place for letters and greeting cards. We suggest that there is such a place, and that they should be used!

Just Do It!

We could go on and on with this. There are so many relationships and circumstances where a few lines on a card would make all the difference, but instead, we suggest you just try it out.

Take a moment to think of a person who most needs to feel a deeper connection with you right now. Perhaps one of your children. Perhaps your spouse. Perhaps the guy in the cubicle next to you. Maybe one of your business partners. Or maybe it's your grandma, who every single year takes a few minutes to focus on you in a handwritten note.

Now it's your turn. Write out a simple thank you, a happy birthday, or a love note. We've tried not to turn this book into too much of a workshop, but there's a time for everything, including letters.

Once you've written your letter, go give it to the intended person, send it in the mail, or drop it off on their desk or at the foot of their bed.

The writing of letters is becoming more and more of a lost art, and that very fact gives more power to this form of communication when someone actively takes the trouble to do it. Although it's "out of date" and perhaps now seen as a bit laborious, don't leave the writing of letters and cards out of your arsenal of communication. You might just be surprised at what they can accomplish.

RULE #31

DON'T FORGET CARRIER PIGEONS AND SMOKE SIGNALS

"There are many mediums of communication: face to face, phone, messages, social networking, letters (remember those?), speaking on stage, carrier pigeons, and smoke signals...."
—CHRIS BRADY

Humor, Just for Fun!

Now for the most effective form of communication of all: carrier pigeons. What is it about sending carrier pigeons that helps communication so much? Obviously, sending a bird with a message in a tiny belt wrapped around its leg is a very personal way to communicate. Very unique.

And of course, if the bird manages to find you, through wind and rain, then you know the commitment level of said bird must match that of his master, and that whoever sent you that bird really cared that you get their message. After all, they must have sent you their most trusted, best-trained bird.

Sending carrier pigeons is important. All people should do it. Send them to your neighbors, to your friends, to your kids at school, and to the guy you just met at the grocery store. (Remember him? Quiz: What's his name?)

Each person deserves to receive a carrier pigeon at one point in his or her life, so if we all send them, hopefully everyone will eventually find real fulfillment.

Again, you should use carrier pigeons for communication. But as with all other mediums, it has its own set of rules or guidelines, so rather than spend all our time trying to convince you how very important it is that you start sending carrier pigeons today, we'll go into more of what it entails. Specifically:

A) You'll need to have some well-trained carrier pigeons.

B) These pigeons must be well cared for, so that they'll want to do what you tell them to.

C) You'll need tiny slips of paper to roll up into scrolls to send with the carrier pigeon. If you don't put the message with the pigeon, you'll waste not only your time but also the time of the person you're sending it to. Not to mention the pigeon himself. Remember to send the scroll with the actual message, because sadly, most pigeons can't actually speak.

SIDEBAR TO READER:

Wait, why are we talking about pigeons again?

D) Be sure to follow all national and local laws and licensing requirements when sending your pigeons. You don't want to get your pigeons arrested. They're only the messengers.

E) All other principles and guidelines of communication should be applied to using carrier pigeons. Especially: *Know Your Audience.*

F) Pigeons are people too. Sort of. But not really. Still, treat them with respect.

G) Don't be too angry if your pigeon takes a bit of time to get back to you. He might have stopped to visit some friends along the way. Or joined a racing team. Or started a business.

H) All the above principles should be applied if and when you communicate with people using drones.

Honestly, we could talk all day about carrier pigeons, but you know as well as we do that they matter and that most communication should be done through the use of carrier pigeons. We previously said that social media has begun to have a huge impact on the world, but it's far less than the impact of carrier pigeons. We should warn you that if you do not use carrier pigeons, you will be very sad.

Pigeons are that important.

In conclusion, we'd like to remind you that you must have a tight bond and a close, caring relationship with your pigeons as well, or they too will be lost to you, and then where will you be?

SIDEBAR TO READER:

Just in case you are a very literal person, note that this entire chapter is just a funny spoof. Except the part below....

The Real Rule #31
At times, use humor, and sometimes communicate just for the fun of it!

PART SEVEN

CHARACTER AND COMMUNICATION

"If you don't know, find out."
—CONFLICT RESOLUTION,
LIFE LEADERSHIP ESSENTIALS SERIES

ALWAYS TRY YOUR "HEARTEST"

*"When it comes to communication,
always try your 'heartest.'"*
—CHRIS BRADY

What Really Matters

Rules, guidelines, principles, mediums of interaction. All of these are facets of communication. But the point of this book is not just to help you get more dates or even to improve your work. It's not only about business success, improved family relationships, or expressing yourself more easily.

Communication is about something a lot more important. Perhaps Chris Brady explained this best when he said that communication is really a matter of the heart. In his words: "Ultimately communication is sharing your heart. It's letting people know your heart. That's really what communication is: getting your heart out there and connecting with other human beings."

Communication shouldn't be about getting the upper hand or taking advantage of others. It should be about what's right and about doing good in the world. When God spoke to Adam and Eve, he used words. And communication has always been, and still is, a key part of participating in God's work.

This may seem too idealistic to some people, but communication is power—and using it well is powerful.

To put it succinctly: your heart must be in the right place if you want to find real success in life.

The Other Side of the Coin

Of course, with that understanding, it is also true that one of the worst situations in life occurs when your heart *is* right, but your communication is wrong—or deficient, or just weak. Just because your intentions are good doesn't mean your execution is excellent as well.

> **Communication shouldn't be about getting the upper hand or taking advantage of others. It should be about what's right and about doing good in the world.**

The rules in this book, though few, will help people who have the right intentions, dreams, and goals and are willing to work hard for what really matters, to raise their communication skills to much higher levels.

It will help them be leaders. It will help them achieve great things.

If you apply these 32 rules of communication, they will work.

They are wise, and they are effective.

Use all of them, or pick and choose the ones that you need to apply right now to improve your work, heal relationships, and live your dreams. Put this book on your reference shelf, and return to it when you need to prepare for a speech, succeed in a new relationship, or strategize personal or team goals to seek and victoriously reach a new milestone.

Each of the 32 rules is important, and together they are powerful.

Indeed, it is very, very important to truly and effectively communicate. As we have discussed in many ways in this book, communication is one of the keys to connection, relationships, success, leadership, happiness, and life.

Conclusion

Of course, it is obvious that to really communicate we must move well beyond baby talk. And although "Point and Grunt" is the classical language used by many babies and rumored to be the dialect of some

> **Genuine greatness demands greater communication.**

cavemen (including the fictional Neanderthal in one *Night at the Museum* movie), it has its limits.

Great leaders need something more. Great families, organizations, communities, and nations need much more. Genuine greatness demands greater communication.

In fact, babies eventually learn that to truly accomplish things that really matter, they have to move beyond pointing, grunting, and temper tantrums in order to really get what they seek from life. And to really connect, humans learn that effective communication is essential.

Apply these 32 rules, and you will see your communication skills consistently improve. Practice and master them, and teach them to loved ones and others you serve and lead. These techniques will really help you. Use them, and use them again and again to become a consistently better and better communicator.

And finally, add to these 32 nuggets of excellence the following:

Communicate so your true heart gets out.
The world needs it.
Communicate with excellence and sincerity.
The world needs *you*.
Communicate to make the world better.
This is who you were born to be.
Communicate the following as far and wide as you can:
Find your life purpose, settle for nothing less,
give your all to achieve it, never stop,
and never give up.
And in the words of Chris Brady,
"Always try your heartest!"

BONUS

What action(s) should you take today?

(please use the space below to write your action plan....)

NOTES

1   Marcus Buckingham, 2005, *The One Thing You Need to Know*, 59.

2   Ibid., 58–60.

3   Ibid., 46–47.

4   See audio "Communication" by Chris Brady.

5   This comparison of Xerox and GE comes from Jerry Useem, "Google's Best Bet," *The Atlantic*, November 2015, 36–38.

6   Ibid., 36–37.

7   Ibid.

8   See Michael Kinsey, "The Anger Games," *Vanity Fair*, February 2015, 75.

9   Matthew Hutson, "Tall Tales," *The Atlantic,* November 2015, 38.

10 Prompted by the popular television commercial, "My Passion Is Puppetry."

11 See Guy Winch, "Harm from a Handheld," Psychology Today, March/April 2015, 37–38.

12 Ibid.

13 Walter Kirn, "If You're Not Paranoid, You're Crazy," *The Atlantic*, November 2015, 100.

14 See Frank Pasquale, *The Black Box Society*, Harvard University Press, 4–7, 30–31, 74–75.

15 See Ibid. See also Kirn, op. cit., 98–106.

16 "The View from the Valley," *The Atlantic*, November 2015, 81.

FINANCIAL FITNESS PROGRAM

Get Out of Debt and Stay Out of Debt!

FREE PERSONAL WEBSITE

SIGN UP AND TAKE ADVANTAGE OF THESE FREE FEATURES:

- Personal website
- Take your custom assessment test
- Build your own profile
- Share milestones and successes with partners and friends
- Post videos and photos
- Receive daily info "nuggets"

FINANCIAL FITNESS BASIC PROGRAM

The first program to teach all three aspects of personal finance: defense, offense, and playing field. Learn the simple, easy-to-apply principles that can help you shore up your resources, get out of debt, and build stability for a more secure future. It's all here, including a comprehensive book, companion workbook, and 8 audios that amplify the teachings from the books.

Also available DIGITALLY!

financialfitnessinfo.com

FINANCIAL FITNESS MASTER CLASS

Buy it once and use it forever! Designed to provide a continual follow-up to the principles learned in the Basic Program, this ongoing educational support offers over 6 hours of video and over 14 hours of audio instruction that walk you through the workbook, step by step. Perfect for individual or group study.
6 videos, 15 audios

FINANCIAL FITNESS TRACK AND SAVE

The Financial Fitness Program teaches you how to get out of debt, build additional streams of income, and properly take advantage of tax deductions. Now, with this subscription, we give you the tools to do so. The Tracker offers mobile expense tracking tools and budgeting software, while the Saver offers you thousands of coupons and discounts to help you save money every day.

THE WEALTH HABITS SERIES

The Wealth Habits series is designed to help you prosper through consistent, ongoing, simple, and enjoyable financial literacy education. You will learn timeless principles about how to better handle your money, and timely commentary on the current economic forces affecting the "playing field" upon which we all must participate. Small doses of information applied consistently over time can produce enormous results through the formation of new and profitable habits. This is what the Wealth Habits series is all about.

The Wealth Habits series will put you in a unique position. You will know something that only a few people in the world know. You will know the principles of financial fitness. You have the power to not only develop financial fitness but also to positively impact the lives of those around you. And the time to act is NOW.

LEARN TO NOT ONLY *SURVIVE*, BUT *THRIVE* DURING TOUGH ECONOMIC TIMES!